At Issue

Male Privilege

Other Books in the At Issue Series

At Issue

| Male Privilege

Anna Wenzel, Book Editor

GREENHAVEN
PUBLISHING

Published in 2020 by Greenhaven Publishing, LLC
353 3rd Avenue, Suite 255, New York, NY 10010

Articles in Greenhaven Publishing anthologies are often edited for length to meet page
requirements. In addition, original titles of these works are changed to clearly present
the main thesis and to explicitly indicate the author's opinion. Every effort is made to
ensure that Greenhaven Publishing accurately reflects the original intent of the authors.
Every effort has been made to trace the owners of the copyrighted material.

Cover image: Lightspring/Shutterstock.com

Library of Congress Cataloging-in-Publication Data

Names: Wenzel, Anna, editor.
Title: Male privilege / Anna Wenzel, book editor.
Description: New York : Greenhaven Publishing, 2020. | Series: At issue |
 Series: First edition | Includes bibliographical references and index. | Audience: Grades
 9–12.
Identifiers: LCCN 2019000382| ISBN 9781534505216 (library bound) | ISBN
 9781534505223 (pbk.)
Subjects: LCSH: Male domination (Social structure)—Juvenile literature. |
 Privilege (Social psychology)—Juvenile literature. | Sex role—Juvenile
 literature.
Classification: LCC HQ1090 .M3287 2020 | DDC 305.31—dc23
LC record available at https://lccn.loc.gov/2019000382

Manufactured in the United States of America

Website: http://greenhavenpublishing.com

Contents

Introduction

In May of 2014, *Time* magazine published an opinion article written by Princeton University student Tal Fortgang titled "Why I'll Never Apologize for My White Male Privilege." The piece condemns the idea that a characteristic like skin color or gender could play a significant role in determining the success an individual achieves in his or her life. While these factors may matter, Fortgang claims, it is ultimately hard work, determination, and intelligence that will get people where they want to be. To illustrate this, he refers to his penniless immigrant grandparents, who despite their destitution were able to make their way in America after enduring the horrors of World War II. To ask someone to "check their privilege," then, is to dismiss their accomplishments and meritocracy itself. Fortgang's article elicited backlash in the form of critical opinion pieces and blog posts. Most of these were written by women (though men authored a fair number, as well) and picked apart Fortgang's argument against privilege. These women claimed to live in a completely different world; they had been passed over for jobs, harassed, and dismissed by their male peers due to their gender. To them, Fortgang did not understand his privilege because, as a white man, his life had never been significantly affected by it. These two perspectives, while not entirely representative of this extensive debate, warrant further investigation on the topic of privilege, its existence, and its reach.

The dialogue concerning male privilege did not begin with the watershed election of 2016 or even with Fortgang's article two years prior, but decades ago. Nevertheless, as the viewpoints in this volume and across the internet demonstrate, male privilege is a contemporary and controversial topic. At its core, privilege is a sociological concept. In terms of its popular usage, the best definition is the one provided by feminist scholar Peggy McIntosh: privilege is a "system of unearned advantages" provided to an individual at birth based on their gender, sexuality, race, and a multitude of other characteristics.[1] Male privilege, specifically, concerns the belief that men are afforded economic, social, and political advantages in most societies. The idea of privilege, while not inherently complex, has been controversial since its first appearance in academic journals of the 1970s. Many men today (and a significant number of women) deny the existence of privilege. On the contrary, they believe that their successes in life were born solely out of their own hard work and personal merits, not because their gender was favored by a system. Even within the feminist camp, which believes this privilege exists, there is discourse over the extent of male privilege as it relates to race, gender identity, and sexuality, though this has fizzled out in recent years as fourth-wave feminism has brought intersectionality to the forefront.

The discussion regarding the existence and extent of privilege is at the crux of this volume. Additionally, readers will become familiarized with real-life experiences that are perceived to be the result of male privilege. The gender pay gap, the preference for sons over daughters across the world, and the distinctly male slant of history taught in schools today are all problems that could be seen as a result of the systemic favor shown to men. On the other hand, as critics of male privilege would argue, they may just be unrelated—if unfortunate—occurrences.

Despite its current relevance, privilege is not a new concept. Marginalized groups have been aware of and fought against their own disadvantages for centuries. Women across the world rallied for equal rights on the historic battlegrounds of public streets and political congresses as early as the nineteenth century. However, it was during the second wave of feminism in the 1970s that the concept of privilege formally entered the academic sphere and the broader social conscience. Male privilege was at the center of this movement, which turned a critical eye towards discrimination against women in the workplace and unequal division of labor within the home. Second-wave scholarship also expanded to include different layers of privilege and oppression, like those based on race and sexuality, and how those affect an individual's experience. These ideas continue to evolve even today.

Much of today's activism concerning the eradication of male privilege is focused on timely topics—the portrayal of women in the media, sexual harassment and assault, and the beauty industry—and for good reason. However, the effects of male privilege on men, especially in the form of toxic masculinity and violence, are underrepresented in much of the literature on the topic. These experiences serve as an important reminder of how male privilege is believed to extend to all spheres of society. Equally vital are the specific types of privilege afforded to men who are members of marginalized groups. For instance, the struggles faced by a black man, who benefits from his gender but not his race, are different from those faced by a black woman, who may experience discrimination based on both her race and her gender. This concept is called intersectionality, as it deals with what occurs at the intersection of multiple disadvantages. It is important to also keep in mind the nuanced differences in gender relations across cultures, as the concept of privilege is strongly entwined with culture and manifests in different ways in different countries, though the overarching themes of oppression and privilege are transferable across borders.

Privilege is a complex, multifaceted concept with a range of viewpoints. The opinions represented in *At Issue: Male Privilege* serve as an entry point by providing a wide selection of pertinent topics. The viewpoints explore the concept of systemic oppression as it relates to male privilege and how male privilege may or may not manifest in society. These are relevant debates taking place online, in schools, and in the streets. Instead of apologizing for privilege, which only ends the conversation, we may strive to better understand what it is and what it is not.

Notes

1. Peggy McIntosh, "White Privilege and Male Privilege," Wellesley College Center for Research on Women, 1998.

1

Male Privilege Requires Action, Not Guilt

Derek Penwill

Derek Penwill is a senior pastor and lecturer of religious studies and comparative humanities at the University of Louisville in Kentucky.

Privilege can be uncomfortable to acknowledge, but shying away from it only serves to perpetuate the oppressive status quo. Rather than ignoring that privilege exists, Derek Penwill argues that we should recognize what characteristics give us a systemic advantage over others (be that our skin color, gender, class, or sexuality) and use it to help those who do not benefit as we do. In this way, privilege can be a tool for liberation rather than oppression.

Lately, I've witnessed a great deal of hand-wringing among white liberals over the issue of privilege. Of course, the most obvious point of contention among the folks on the left is how to convince their non-liberal white friends that straight white people possess any number of privileges in virtue of their "straightness" and their "whiteness." Such a rhetorical exercise too often proves futile, however.

"What do you mean I'm privileged? I know a lot of minorities who have a lot more than I do."

"Privilege? My parents worked four jobs each, just so we could have an orange in our Christmas stocking. Don't talk to me about privilege."

"How to Use Your White, Cisgender, Male Privilege for Good," Derek Penwell. Originally published on The Good Men Project, September 19, 2018. Reprinted by permission.

"I don't accept the premise of privilege. We live in a democracy, where everyone has the same opportunities I do."

"Talking about privilege only divides the country. We need to move on."

A few thoughts occur to me:

- Although we're used to talking about it in this way, "privilege," in this sense, doesn't necessarily equal "rich."
- Saying that privilege doesn't exist because everyone has the same opportunities is like running in a 100-meter dash where everyone else but you is wearing a lead vest; you may be running the same distance, but it's obviously not the same race for everyone else.
- Talking about "moving on" from conversations about privilege is itself a privilege. It's like being in a car accident where everybody but you is severely injured, and then trying to get your fellow passengers to quit whining and get over it because you did.

Progressives should bear in mind that any change in perspective on the part of those who don't feel privileged will not come easily, that if we could just find the perfect argument …

But another, perhaps more personal issue white liberals deal with is guilt over their own privilege. They know that the engines of their socio-economic futures came with turbochargers as standard equipment; for everyone else, it's a costly upgrade. Consequently, white liberals wonder what to do about the fact that they come specially equipped to win the road rally our culture stages.

In order to begin to think about it, however, it's important to point out that privilege is a set of benefits conferred on you without your consent. Nobody gets to ask to be born white or male. There's no pre-natal menu where you get to choose your sexual orientation or gender identity. You don't pick your parents, your eye color, your eventual height, or whether or not you have a cleft chin or fetching eyelashes. All these things are accidents of birth.

Consequently, feeling guilty for facets of your identity you were born with, though a fairly common response, is pointless. You can't apologize your way out of being white, or male, or straight, or cisgender. If you are some or all those things, you're stuck with them. So, quit feeling guilty about things over which you have no control.

Having said that, however, there are things you can control. You have the chance every morning to decide how you're going to trade on those advantages you've been given. You can try to forget about them, try to fool yourself into thinking that they don't grant you any benefits. But the thing is, if you can forget the constitutive aspects of your identity, you're taking advantage of a privilege other people don't possess. You can't forget if you're black or woman or Latinx or gay or transgender or disabled because of the simple fact that the world won't let you. You are reminded regularly that your status is a negative impression of "normal."

Let me see if I can be clearer. Aristotle infamously believed that women were deformed men. Women cannot produce semen, which Aristotle believed carried a whole human being, a homunculus. A woman's femaleness, therefore, was negatively defined against a man's maleness by what she lacked. In other words, a man was the perfect expression of nature, the standard of full humanness by which all of humanity was measured. The hierarchy was established with the Western male at the top of the food chain.

Almost nobody would say that about women now, but we often act as though it were true. Women are the "weaker sex," who need a protector and provider, so that they may be made "whole." Where men are "rational," women are "emotional," lacking the executive function that sets men apart.

We do the same thing with race, sexual orientation, gender expression, disability: We negatively define them against the standard of able white, heterosexual, cis-gender males, from which any deviation is unwittingly viewed as a defect. In other words, everyone else always has to be aware of that which they "lack," having to exert extraordinary amounts of energy proving they can compensate for the deficit, make it a non-factor. They get no benefit of the doubt.

Black men, for example, have to "prove" that they're not a threat on the street or in the store.

Women have to work "twice as hard" as any man to prove their competence on the job.

LGBTQ people have to "prove" that they're not deviants, whose very presence is threatening to children or women in bathrooms.

Straight white guys get the benefit of the doubt. The assumptions always favor them. Generally, they have to "prove" that they are threatening and incompetent before they're treated that way. They can walk through the day, for instance, without worrying whether people suspect they're about to do harm or that they're unable to do the job they've trained for. Most of the time, it never occurs to them to think anyone is suspicious of them for anything … unless they're actually doing something suspicious.

That is privilege. It's not a moral failure of the recipient to have been given these benefits. At present, it's just the way our culture works.

So, the right question isn't, "Should I feel guilty for being born this way?" A better question is, "Having concluded that I have these advantages, how will I use them to try to create a world in which everyone shares them with me?"

People of privilege need to begin to pursue a just world, challenging the assumptions about who's benign and who's competent. They need to leverage those advantages, both to provide access to those who don't yet enjoy it, as well as to help confront the prejudices of race, gender identity and expression, ability, and sexual orientation that our culture takes for granted.

2

Gender and Privilege in the Workplace

Ariane Hegewisch and Emma Williams-Baron

Ariane Hegewisch is the Program Director of Employment and Earnings at the Institute for Women's Policy Research (IWPR) and a scholar-in-residence at American University. Emma Williams-Baron is a policy and data analyst at IWPR and an assistant editor for the Journal of Women, Politics & Policy.

Equal treatment of men and women in the workplace was one of the central issues during the second wave of feminism of the 1960s. However, Ariane Hegewisch and Emma Williams-Baron argue that although activists have made great strides toward workplace equality since the 1960s, the present pay gap between white men and women of all colors could indicate that male privilege continues to cause unfair practices in the workplace. This gap is even more pronounced for women of color, indicating that race and gender are both variables in the pay gap.

The gender wage gap in weekly earnings for full-time workers in the United States did not improve between 2016 and 2017. In 2017, the ratio of women's to men's median weekly full-time earnings was 81.8 percent, a decrease of 0.1 percentage points since 2016, when the ratio was 81.9 percent, leaving a wage gap of 18.2 percentage points, nearly the same as the 18.1 percentage points in 2016. Women's median weekly earnings for full-time

"The Gender Wage Gap: 2017 Earnings Differences by Race and Ethnicity," by Ariane Hegewisch, Emma Williams-Baron, Institute for Women's Policy Research, March 7, 2018. Reprinted by permission.

work were $770 in 2017 compared with $941 for men. Adjusting for inflation, women's and men's earnings increased by the same amount, 0.7 percent, since 2016.[1]

Another measure of the wage gap, the ratio of women's and men's median annual earnings for full-time, year-round workers, was 80.5 percent in 2016 (data for 2017 are not yet available). An earnings ratio of 80.5 percent means that the gender wage gap for full-time, year-round workers is 19.5 percent.

The gender earnings ratio for full-time, year-round workers, which includes self-employed workers, tends to be slightly lower than the ratio for weekly earnings (which excludes the self-employed and earnings from annual bonuses, and includes full-time workers who work only part of the year). Both earnings ratios are for full-time workers only; if part-time workers were included, the ratios of women's to men's earnings would be even lower, as women are more likely than men to work reduced schedules, often in order to manage childrearing and other caregiving work.

Since 1980, when weekly earnings data were first collected, the weekly gender earnings ratio has risen from just 64.2 percent to 81.8 percent now. Most of the progress towards gender equality took place in the 1980s and 1990s. In the past ten years (2008 to 2017), the weekly gender wage gap narrowed by just 2.0 percentage points, compared with 3.9 percentage points in the previous ten years (1998 to 2007), and with 4.4 percentage points in the ten years prior to that (1988 to 1997). Progress in closing the gender earnings gap based on median annual earnings has also slowed considerably. If the pace of change in the annual earnings ratio were to continue at the same rate as it has since 1985, it would take until 2059 for women and men to reach earnings parity.[2]

Earnings Differences by Gender, Race, and Ethnicity

Women of all major racial and ethnic groups earn less than men of the same group, and also earn less than White men. Hispanic workers have lower median weekly earnings than White, Black, and Asian workers. Hispanic women's median weekly earnings in 2017 were $603 per week of full-time work, only 62.2 percent of White men's median weekly earnings, but 87.4 percent of the median weekly earnings of Hispanic men (because Hispanic men also have low earnings). The median weekly earnings of Black women were $657, only 67.7 percent of White men's earnings, but 92.5 percent of Black men's median weekly earnings. Primarily because of higher rates of educational attainment for both genders, Asian workers have higher median weekly earnings than White, Black or Hispanic workers (the highest of any group studied). Asian women's earnings are 93.0 percent of White men's earnings, but only 74.8 percent of Asian men's earnings. White women earn 81.9 percent of what White men earn, very close to the ratio for all women to all men, because White workers remain the largest group in the labor force.

Women and men of the largest racial and ethnic groups, besides Asian women and men, saw increases in median weekly earnings between 2016 and 2017.[3] White women's real earnings increased by 1.6 percent, Hispanic women's by 0.8 percent, and Black women's by 0.4 percent. Asian women saw a decrease in median weekly earnings of 2.0 percent. Asian, Hispanic, and White men's earnings increased (by 2.7 percent, 1.9 percent, and 0.9 percent, respectively), while Black men's earnings fell by 3.2 percent. Earnings for a full-time week of work leave Hispanic women well below, and Hispanic men and Black women not much above, the qualifying income threshold for receipt of food stamps of $615 per week for a family of four.[4]

Women's lower earnings are due to a number of factors, including lower earnings in occupations done mainly by women; lack of paid family leave and subsidized child care; and discrimination in compensation, recruitment, and hiring.[5] Measures to improve the quality of jobs held mainly by women, tackle occupational segregation, enforce equal pay and employment opportunities, and improve work family benefits for all workers, will help the incomes of women and their families grow and strengthen the economy.[6]

Notes

1. 2016 earnings were converted into 2017 dollars using the Consumer Price Index Series (CPI-U) , US Bureau of Labor Statistics [https://www.bls.gov/cpi/tables/supplemental-files/historical-cpi-u-201801.pdf] (accessed March 2018).

2. Institute for Women's Policy Research. November 2017. "Women's Median Earnings as a Percent of Men's, 1985-2016 (Full-time, Year-Round Workers) with Projection for Pay Equity, by Race/Ethnicity." IWPR Quick Figures #Q066 [https://iwpr.org/publications/womens-median-earnings-1985-2016/] (accessed March 2018).

3. According to data provided by the US Bureau of Labor Statistics, changes in earnings between 2016 and 2017 were statistically significant for White women and men; for other groups, with smaller survey sample sizes, 2017 earnings were within the margin of error compared to 2016 data.

4. To qualify for food stamps, the income of a household of four must be at or below 130 percent of the federal poverty level; in 2016/17 this earning threshold was $2,665 per month, corresponding to $615 per week (USDA Food and Nutrition Service. 2017). *Supplemental Nutrition Assistance Program (SNAP)*. On the internet at [http://www.fns.usda.gov/snap/eligibility] (accessed March 2018).

5. Blau, Francine D., and Lawrence Kahn. 2016. "The Gender Wage Gap: Extent, Trends, and Explanations," NBER Working Paper No. 21913. [http://www.nber.org/papers/w21913] (accessed March 2018).

6. Council for Economic Advisers. 2015. "Gender Pay Gap: Recent Trends and Explanations." Issue Brief. The White House [https://www.whitehouse.gov/sites/default/files/docs/equal_pay_issue_brief_final.pdf] (accessed March 2016); Institute for Women's Policy Research. February 2016. "The Economic Impact of Equal Pay by State." IWPR #R468 [http://www.iwpr.org/publications/pubs/the-economic-impact-of-equal-pay-by-state] (accessed March 2018).

3

How Race and Gender Affect Equal Pay

Elise Gould and Adriana Kugler

Elise Gould is a senior economist at the Economic Policy Institute. Adriana Kugler is a professor at the McCourt School of Public Policy at Georgetown University.

Out of all groups, Latina women suffer the most under the pay gap. Elise Gould and Adriana Kugler find that Latina women, like black women, face discrimination for both their race and their gender, especially when it comes to the workplace. Statistically, Latina women tend to occupy lower-paying jobs, but even in higher-paying professions they often only earn a fraction of what their white, male coworkers do. This viewpoint takes a closer look at the extent to which women of color experience a pay disadvantage.

November 2nd is Latina Equal Pay Day, the day that marks how long into 2017 a Latina would have to work in order to be paid the same wages as her white male counterpart was paid last year. That's just over 10 months longer, meaning that Latina workers had to work all of 2016 and then this far—to November 2nd—into 2017 to get paid the same as white non-Hispanic men did in 2016. Unfortunately, Hispanic women are subject to a double pay gap—an ethnic pay gap and a gender pay gap. On average, Latina workers are paid only 67 cents on the dollar relative to white

"Latina Workers Have to Work 10 Months Into 2017 to Be Paid the Same as White Non-Hispanic Men in 2016," by Elise Gould and Adriana Kugler, Economic Policy Institute, November 1, 2017. Reprinted by permission.

non-Hispanic men, even after controlling for education, years of experience, and location.

The wage gap between Latina workers and white non-Hispanic male workers persists across the wage distribution, within occupations, and among those with the same amount of education. The 10th percentile Latina wage identifies the wage at which 10 percent of Latina workers earn less while 90 percent of Latina workers earn more. At the 10th percentile, Latina workers are paid $8.53 per hour, or 85 percent of the white male wage at the 10th percentile ($10.03 per hour). This wage gap—15 percent—is the smallest the gap gets, likely due to the wage floor set by the minimum wage. The gap rises to 41 percent at the middle of the wage distribution, and to 55 percent at the 95th percentile. That means that even the best paid Latinas are paid *half* as much as the best paid white non-Hispanic men.

Latinas are, thus, vastly over-represented in low-wage jobs and relatively under-represented in high-wage jobs. In fact, Latinas' *median* wages are just above those of white men's 10th percentile wage. In other words, *nearly half* of all Latina workers are paid less than the 10th percentile white male worker. Meanwhile, by comparing the white male median to the 80th percentile Latinas' wages, you can see that more than half of white men are paid over $20 an hour while fewer than 20 percent of Latinas are. At the high end, only 1-in-20 Latina workers are paid more than white male workers at the 80th percentile.

Much of these differences are grounded in the presence of occupational segregation. Latina workers are far more likely to be found in certain low-wage professions than white men are (and less common in high-wage professions). But, even in professions with more Latina workers, they still are paid less on average than their white male colleagues. In every one of them, white men, on average, are paid more than their Latina counterparts.

Since Hispanic women continue to be over-represented in low-wage jobs, policies that lift wages at the bottom will have a significant impact on their wages. An increase of the federal minimum wage to $15 by 2024 would affect more than 1-in-5 Latina workers.

While some (incorrectly) argue that Latinas are choosing lower-paid professions, further education clearly does not close their sizable wage gaps with white non-Hispanic men. As Hispanic women increase their educational attainment, their pay gap with white men actually *increases*. The largest dollar gap (more than $17 an hour), occurs for workers with more than a college degree. Even Hispanic women with an advanced degree earn less than white men who only have a bachelor's degree. That statistic bears repeating. White non-Hispanic men with only a college degree are paid, on average, $7.53 *more* than Latinas with an advanced degree!

Regardless of their place in the wage distribution, their level of educational attainment, or their occupation, Latinas are paid less than their white male counterparts. The ongoing gender and ethnic discrimination faced by Hispanic women means that ten months into 2017, Latinas finally reach the same typical pay as non-Hispanic white men earned last year. That means that over a 30 year span, Latinas would have to work another 25 years for them to earn the same over their working life as non-Hispanic white men.

There is a lot of work to be done to improve the standard of living for the families of Latinas. More educational attainment and access to better quality education would certainly help to improve the Latinas' chances to move up the job ladder and get better paid jobs. However, this is not the whole story, since even after controlling for education the wage gap remains very large. Offering and facilitating access to occupations that are higher paid will also move Latinas up the occupational ladder. Here too, however, we find that even within the same occupations, Latinas fare worse. Lastly, it is important to improve equal pay for equal work provisions so that those women who do have the same education, the same occupation and are equally qualified in the workplace are not paid less or driven away from moving up to these more challenging positions.

4

Male Privilege in Family Life

Sarah Schoppe-Sullivan

Sara Schoppe-Sullivan is a professor of human sciences and psychology at Ohio State University. Her research interests include coparenting, the roles of fathers in the family system, and the effects of children's characteristics and behavior on family relationships.

The domestic sphere is a less visible area for male privilege, but Sarah Schoppe-Sullivan argues that it continues to be a place where women shoulder a disproportionate amount of work with little recognition. Over the past few decades, fathers have taken a more active role in family life. However, Schoppe-Sullivan finds that as parenting itself has become more intensive and child-centered, the extra labor almost always falls on the mother, whose contributions to familial and domestic life continue to be taken for granted.

On Jan. 21, in a collective demonstration of historic proportions, millions of women marched in Washington, D.C. and other cities around the world in support of key policy issues such as reproductive rights, equal pay for equal work and support for balancing work and family.

These marches demonstrated the empowerment of women and a widespread commitment to ensuring that women's rights are furthered—and not eroded—by policymakers. But policy is not the only arena that affects women's freedoms and well-being.

If equality begins at home, how much progress has been made toward equality in parenting?

The day after the march, *The New York Times* published an article that described a scene in Montclair, New Jersey, showing what happened when women were absent from town. The article narrated how women's absence resulted in empty yoga classes, Starbucks cafes populated by men and hapless fathers struggling to juggle children's weekend schedules.

In other words, as its critics pointed out, the article reinforced the outdated notion that mothers are the primary parents and fathers are (at best) mere helpers and incapable of caring for children independently.

My research focuses on the sharing of parenting between mothers and fathers in dual-earner couples—a group that is most likely to hold gender egalitarian beliefs. In this group, successfully balancing work and family makes some degree of shared parenting necessary.

My research and that of others shows that even though significant progress has been made toward gender equality in parenting, more subtle inequalities remain. Many fathers—even those in the households most likely to have progressive views on parenting—have not achieved equality with mothers in key areas.

Men's Parenting Time Has Increased, But Women's Has Too

It is true that today's fathers are more involved in parenting children than ever before. Over the past half-century, fathers in America nearly tripled their child care time from 2.5 hours per week in 1965 to seven hours per week in 2011.

But, over this period, women's parenting time too has increased—from 10 hours per week in 1965 to 14 hours per week in 2011. This has resulted in a smaller but persistent gap in the time mothers and fathers spend on parenting.

This gap starts in the earliest months of parenthood. Using detailed daily records of new parents' activities, my team's research has shown that working mothers take on a greater share of the child care burden for a new baby than do fathers. In fact, new mothers allocated twice as much of their available time to routine child care activities than fathers.

When considering time spent in child care plus time spent in housework and working for pay, the birth of a baby increased mothers' total workload by 21 hours per week. In contrast, fathers' total workload increased by only 12.5 hours per week. This represents a 70 percent greater increase in workload for women compared to men.

These differences cannot be explained away by differences in paid work hours or breastfeeding.

Mothers Face Intense Parenting Pressure

So, the question remains, why hasn't fathers' greater involvement substituted for mothers' involvement, thus reducing the parenting burden on women?

What has happened is that middle-class families now follow the norm of "intensive parenting," which dictates that parenting should be child-centered, guided by expert advice and costly in terms of time, money and emotional investment in order to produce the most successful child possible.

Picture modern parents scouring bookstores for the latest parenting manual and preschool math workbooks, fretting over their toddler's picky eating habits and overloading their weekly schedules with children's activities and playdates. This pressure to parent intensively does not fall equally on middle-class mothers and fathers, however. Because motherhood remains an idealized role, it is mothers who experience the greatest pressure to meet these unrealistic parenting standards.

Mothers who feel intense pressure to invest heavily in their children may also be reluctant to give up control over parenting. What ends up happening is that fathers spend less time in sole charge of their children. Research on parenting time shows that women are in sole charge of their children for nearly one-third of their time whereas men only for about 8 percent of their time.

Thus, even fathers who are highly involved coparents may experience parenting primarily in the company of children's mothers and more rarely on their own.

Mothers Do More Multitasking

Another area in which subtle, persistent inequality exists is multitasking—especially doing several unpaid work activities (e.g., housework and child care) at the same time.

Mothers multitask more than fathers do. A recent study showed the size of this difference: mothers in dual-earner families spent 10 more hours per week multitasking than did fathers. When fathers are parenting solo, they may be focusing on the basics: making sure children are fed, getting children to/from activities, etc. In contrast, when mothers are parenting solo, they may be taking care of the basics while also getting housework done and/or doing paid work.

Although multitasking may be efficient, frequent multitasking contributes to greater day-to-day stress for mothers compared to fathers. Mothers who did more multitasking at home felt more frustrated, irritated and anxious. They said they felt more often rushed or pressed for time.

Thus, if fathers are less likely to multitask child care and housework, some women may have returned from the march to weekend laundry or grocery shopping left undone, thus beginning the new work week with an additional burden.

Mothers Do More Managing and Organizing

Intensive parenting requires strong dedication to managing children's activities, organizing schedules and making appointments—part of the so-called "worry work" of parenting.

This aspect of parenting is especially challenging to study, because much of this work takes place inside the parent's head.

Research that has surveyed or interviewed parents about who takes responsibility for the managerial and organizational aspects of parenting indicates that mothers take greater responsibility than fathers.

In fact, fathers' involvement in this component of parenting has lagged behind gains in their direct involvement in caring for their children. In other words, mothers are more likely to make child care arrangements, schedule doctors' appointments and sign the permission slips. Mothers remember and mothers remind.

Perhaps some mothers who traveled to the D.C. march might want to recall, how many reminders and to-do lists for children and fathers did they need to leave behind? And how many text messages were exchanged with fathers about where to find a missing sport or dance class accessory?

The truth, as made evident through *The New York Times* article, is: We still have a way to go to achieve equality in parenting.

5

Violence and Masculinity

Colleen Clemens

Colleen Clemens is the director of women's and gender studies and an associate professor of non-Western literature at Kutztown University in Pennsylvania. She is also a co-host on the podcast Inside254.

From a young age, parents, teachers, and classmates often teach boys that being aggressive, unemotional, and sometimes even violent towards others—especially girls—is normal behavior for their sex. Colleen Clemens argues that this pedagogy manifests later on in life as toxic masculinity, and it harms both men and women throughout their teen and adult lives. In order to put an end to widespread violent behavior among men, boys must be taught that it is not acceptable or expected of them to behave in that way.

I am on the playground with my young daughter. A boy, a stranger, knocks her over, leaving my child crying in the sand. The mother tells me, "Boys will be boys" and neglects to ask her son to apologize to my child.

We have all heard it: on the playground, in a teacher conference, in the faculty room. In my 20 years as a teacher, I have heard "boys will be boys" more times than I can count, most often during discussions of a boy's behavior. But when we unpack this comment, we see that it perpetuates negative ideas about what we expect from our boys, particularly when it comes to aggression.

"Say No to 'Boys Will Be Boys,'" by Colleen Clemens, Southern Poverty Law Center, December 21, 2017. Reprinted with permission of Teaching Tolerance, a project of the Southern Poverty Law Center, www.tolerance.org.

First, the phrase implies that boys are biologically wired to be violent, rough and tumble—and that they should be excused from any consequences for that behavior. When our culture buys into the idea that the "male sex" (not gender) is hardwired for violence, we can excuse behaviors that hurt others physically and emotionally.

Despite what '90s self-help books may say, when discussing sex (not gender), men are not from Mars, and women aren't from Venus. Neuroscientist Lise Eliot has done extensive work to show that the brains of girls and boys are not all that different. Such biological essentialism argues that "boys will be boys" because their biology naturally leans toward violence and aggression. When such a belief is upheld in a classroom, it contributes to a toxic foundation to boys' senses of self.

Second, this phrase—and the other two I address below—replicates the idea that there is only one way to be a boy. If we shift the discussion from sex (the biological elements) to gender (the psychic elements), we find the freedom to disrupt this one-size-fits-all way to be a boy.

Understanding how people identify allows us to define gender differently. If we think about gender as distinct from sex, as the way someone feels as opposed to something that is biological, we can no longer excuse negative behaviors in or out of the classroom with the line, "Boys will be boys." As The Good Men Project reminds us, toxic masculinity is "a narrow and repressive description of manhood, designating manhood as defined by violence, sex, status and aggression." Let's give boys more credit by deleting "boys will be boys" from our conversations.

"He Does That Because He Likes You"

I am in junior high school. A boy snaps my bra in the hallway. When I inform the teacher, she tells me he did it because "he likes me," and he doesn't know any other way to tell me.

Toxic masculinity relies on notions that boys are incapable of expressing themselves through means other than violence. When we dismiss boys' aggression as evidence of affection, as with "boys will be boys," we sell all children short. To girls, the message is, "That violent act to which you did not consent means that he feels love for you." And the message to boys is, "When you feel an emotion, you should express it through violence."

This kind of thinking implies that it's strange for boys to hav[e] feelings of love that are disconnected from feelings of violence. In a time when our country is coming to terms with the pervasiveness of sexual assault and sexual harassment, parents and educators must think carefully about what we tell our children.

When we tell our boys it's normal to show that they like someone by hurting them, we don't just excuse toxic masculinity— we encourage it. We are effectively not teaching our children what safe and consensual relationships look like at the moments when they are just starting to come of age sexually.

"Locker Room Talk"

I am an adult on a talk show discussing politics and sexual assault. A man tells me that grabbing women by their genitalia is "locker room talk." I tell him that I have more faith in men than he must have.

For many secondary students, school is where they find themselves in a locker room for the first time. Because they are separated by sex and/or gender, locker rooms are often regarded as spaces where people can "let loose" and "be themselves." For students, locker rooms can become places to study what it means to be one's sex. (I wish I could say "gender," but locker and bathroom laws still need to be legislated fairly in many states.)

Because, as a woman, I am prohibited from the space of a men's locker room, it becomes mysterious, something men can define. I can't know what men say in men's locker rooms. But I can know that when the phrase "locker room talk" is deployed to excuse aggressive sexual acts that do not involve consent, we as a culture are using a more advanced version of "boys will be boys."

I respect the boys and men in my life too much to have such low expectations for them. Their biology does not demand that they become assaulters. And their biology does not necessitate that they speak about women in vulgar ways. Our constructed beliefs about masculinity teach them that, in order to "man up," they must perform their masculinity in aggressive ways—or have their masculinity questioned.

The boys in our homes and classrooms deserve better, and we, as the adults in their lives, must work to dismantle the cultural messages and societal structures that promote toxic masculinity. We have a lot of work ahead, but we can begin one phrase at a time.

6

What Is Misogynynoir?

TaLynn Kel

TaLynn Kel is a writer, public speaker, and host of the New Wakanda *podcast. Her work focuses on bringing light to racism, sexism, ableism, and fatphobia in popular culture. She has been published in the* Huffington Post, *BlackScifi.com,* and Everyday Feminism.

Women of color exist at the intersection of their race and gender and can face discrimination for both. In this viewpoint, author TaLynn Kel focuses on the experiences of black women, who she argues have been excluded by both the feminist and civil rights movements, finding that neither has been able to sufficiently represent them. This particular type of prejudice against black women is called misogynynoir, and it is another manifestation of male privilege. Kel claims that instead of helping to uplift and advocate for black women, black men have ignored the unique struggles of the women in their community and done little to include them in the endeavor for racial equality.

Y'all on ALL my nerves. I honestly didn't think I had any unbothered nerves left but then some Black men proved me wrong. Repeatedly.

So, for the ones in the back struggling with this concept: In the fight against white supremacy, you are not neutral! You are not neutral. You cannot be neutral, so stop pretending you are.

"To the Black Men Who Think They Are Neutral But Really Support White Patriarchal Supremacy ..." by TaLynn Kel, June 19, 2018. Reprinted by permission.

As much as you want to believe that you can live a day without politics, you can't. You can't because you are a Black man. A BLACK man. Your skin color makes you political. That means that everything you say and everything you do is political. And if you didn't know, now you do.

I have had too many discussions where you act like the sh*t going on in this country doesn't affect you, where you think that by saying nothing, you're not agreeing to anything. Except when it comes to oppression, saying nothing actually is saying that whatever wrongdoing is happening, you're cool with it. It's saying that you don't give enough of a f*ck to consider what it's costing somebody else because you *think* it's not costing you anything. It makes you complicit and it means you support white supremacy.

I've had discussions where you refuse to hold space for Black people. I've listened to you talk about turning the other cheek in the face of racial and gendered injustice. I've been in Facebook groups that have insisted that all we talk about is our fandoms without politics, as if politics isn't the air we breathe, the schools we attend, the jobs we get, the medical care we have access to … as if politics doesn't impact every part of our lives in every way and has for centuries. I've had to exit so many groups run by Black men who insist that they don't live a politicized existence; who push this illusion of neutrality and wield that sh*t with surgical precision when it comes to silencing voices raised against oppression.

I see it when you continue to support openly anti-Black, misogynoiristic artists like Kanye. You support men with a history of violence against Black women like R Kelly, Chris Brown, Nas … men who have never acknowledged the horrible sh*t they've done and feel entitled to their continued popularity despite the inhumane cruelty they inflicted. I watch you play the "separate the art from the artist" game while simultaneously punishing Black women for daring to criticize their behaviors.

You follow your misogynoiristic bullsh*t "leaders" like Tariq Nasheed, Boyce Watkins, Umar Johnson, and Tommy Sotermeyer who rise to popularity by sh*tting on Black women. You state that "both sides" need to be heard. That conversation's questioning our humanity deserve space and respect. You have reason after reason for why it's ok to slander Black women and Blackness while you knee-jerk defend whiteness as though you were born to it. It's almost as though you fear losing the tiny bit of power patriarchy grants you, so to prove your worth, you double-down on oppressing Black women, making us your unwilling sacrifice as you grovel for power.

You hold space for whiteness in what should be all Black spaces. You cape for their rights as if it doesn't curtail yours. I constantly struggle to understand how you don't see yourself in the protests of Black women … in the need for our own spaces with our own rules that reject whiteness in all forms. Instead, you fight to silence those discussions. You fight to engage in faux dominance and leadership, when really your power isn't the result of your work, but is, instead, your co-opting of the violent tools that were used to subjugate you. And because the illusion is more attractive than the reality, you cling to oppressive actions, to violence, to lies … lies that say you are entitled to exploiting and subjugating women and deserve all the space to reform your ways despite the damage you've inflicted.

I watch you undermining the work of Black women, stealing credit and accolades instead of using the little bit of male privilege to elevate others. You engage in the practice of hoarding power, just like your oppressors, and give access based on how well women please your eye and pander to your ego. You boast of the subtle and obvious ways you try to superimpose your name over mine and other Black women. We just struggle with how quickly someone who is in the trenches with us will f*ck us over for an ego boost or white approval, then call us angry for resisting, traitors for protecting ourselves, and bedwenches for divesting from your abuse to find love that includes mutual respect.

We sit in these white spaces that constantly tell us we don't belong and watch you try to erase your Blackness to appease the white eyes observing you. You push politics out the conversation, never acknowledging that you are erasing your Black experience with it. You tell yourself that obvious racist sh*t isn't racist. That racist art isn't racist. "He's an alien," you say. "You're reading too much into it," you say. "Stop making this about your 'feminist agenda,'" you say as you make yourself into the self-appointed gatekeepers to geekdom, assuming your penis automatically makes you an expert and excuses you from the myriad of toxic, damaging sh*t you do. You stand beside known abusers and protect them. You hang with your trash, abusive friends and co-sign on their bullsh*t because you think your proximity to them [will] give you some of the power you crave.

You can't separate the abuser from the abuse. You can't separate the artist from the art. They literally ARE the art they create. If you can't acknowledge that their trauma and abuse is a part of the sh*t they make, then you are lying to yourself. It's cool that sports/cosplay/photography/books/tv/movies/ are an escape for you, but you need to admit that these things are problematic because their creators are problematic; otherwise you're just perpetuating and sugar-coating dangerous, toxic sh*t. When you fight for white people to depict a future that excludes Black people, you're advocating for your own genocide.

Kill the blinders and end the bullsh*t. Stop helping create and perpetuate anti-Black spaces. Stop pretending that if you only talk shit about women and n*ggers then it's okay, cuz the truth you're refusing to see is that you are the n*gger tap dancing to their song and doing their work for them.

It hurts. I know it hurts. Every time you have to think about it, it stabs you. And sure, all this awareness and thinking about how art embodies the values of its creators makes sh*t less fun. Believe me, I know. I know how it feels to never see yourself or people who look like you in the future. I know how it feels to be told that wanting to be seen ruins the artist's ability to create their art. I know how it feels to read/watch/hear things created by people who don't think I should exist. And while white people erase us from their narratives, you erase Black women from yours.

I struggle to reconcile my erasure from the works of Black men; that Black women's voices, bodies, beauty, sexuality, humanity, and lives are often placed on the alter to be sacrificed for the approval of the white gaze. We are used by Black men to further the agenda of white supremacy and anti-Blackness ... to appease your oppressors and further your pseudo-liberation aspirations. You are living a lie drenched in the blood of Black women and you aren't even strong enough to admit it, much less change it.

You need to change it. Stop lying to yourselves about your desire to appease whiteness. Stop lying to yourself about the respect you claim to have for Black women. Own your hate, recognize that it's self-hate, and start working on fixing that sh*t cuz it's killing all of us. Whiteness exists solely to exploit and erase you and until you understand that, everything you do to succeed in their game is a path to your self-destruction.

Do better.

7

How Gender Impacts the Study of History

National Women's History Museum

The National Women's History Museum is a nonprofit, online educational resource that seeks to uncover and highlight women's vital contributions to history.

In the United States, school curricula rarely afford women equal space in the classroom, particularly in the subject of history. This imbalance, which the National Women's History Museum has statistically measured, means that the roles of men in history are over-emphasized, while the contributions of women, people of color, and LGBTQ+ individuals receive little to no attention. When they are present, women's roles in history are often limited to domestic ones. Consequently, the authors claim, young, heterosexual, cis-gender (a person whose gender identification conforms to one's gender at birth), white men are afforded the privilege of seeing themselves represented in school textbooks, while members of any other group do not receive the same treatment.

*W*here are the Women? examines the status of women's history in state level social studies standards. States have devised sets of learning standards that describe what students are expected to know and be able to do at specific stages of education. The report and analysis finds that women's experiences and stories are not well integrated into US state history standards. The lack of representation and context in state-level materials presupposes

"Where Are the Women?" National Women's History Museum. Reprinted by permission.

that women's history is even less represented at the classroom level. This implies that women's history is not important.

Project Methodology

The Museum's project team read the social studies standards for each state and the District of Columbia. Project staff highlighted every standard that referred to a woman or a topic associated with women. Each standard was copied into a database. Researchers—following guidance from the Museum's advisory council of scholars, public historians, and educators—reviewed the database entries to ensure that the selected standards met the project's definitions of history about women. In the final step, researchers counted the number of times that women's names and key terms occurred within the standards. The analysis describes the way that women's history is characterized in US K-12 social studies standards. It suggests that women are excluded because the standards' historiographical framework preferences male-oriented exceptional leadership while over-emphasizing women's domestic roles.

Interesting Findings

Individual Women

One hundred seventy-eight individual women are named in state standards. Fifteen women are named more than ten times in standards. Individual women listed in standards are usually those who achieved a level of national or regional name recognition for their activities.

Women by Race

Since the new history movement that began in the 1960s, coinciding with modern rights movements, many states include the history of marginalized groups in standards. Women as a group are often characterized as one of these marginalized groups along with ethnic minority groups and the working class. Non-elite, non-white women who appear in the standards are most often associated with the history of their marginalized groups. The 178 women listed in standards occupy the following racial distribution: 63% White, 25% African American, 8% Hispanic, 4% Native American/Native Alaskan, 0% Asian American or Pacific Islander.

The distribution of women by racial category reflects the emphasis on standards on protest movements. The first women's rights movement in the nineteenth century arose as elite, white women challenged social, economic, political, and cultural definitions of women's roles. Many of these women rose to national prominence by effective use of the media. Elite, white women who had the most access to resources to advance their causes are over represented in the standards. African American women are most often connected to the Abolitionist and modern Civil Rights movements, which are widely included in standards. Other rights movements like disability rights, Native American rights, LGBTQ, or migrant labor movements are less frequently included in standards and, when they are, in less detail. Therefore, they have fewer corresponding biographical entries.

Topics About Women

State standards divide social studies into topic areas. While women occasionally appear by name under topics, more often women are listed as a group. In some cases, topics are understood to be about women or inclusive of women—i.e. Seneca Falls Convention, family, or the home front. With the guidance of the Museum's Advisory Council, the project team culled a list of terms from the data that assumes standards writers intended the standards to be inclusive of women's roles and activities. We found 1,975 mentions of women, women's history, and women's roles within all state standards.

The standards overwhelmingly emphasize women in their domestic roles.

The team did not count the total number of standards, men by name, or the number of topics about men. Therefore, the project cannot determine the percentage of women's topics relative to all topics within all state standards.

What We Learned

- Standards prioritize listing women of accomplishment, which reflects the standards' overall tendency to celebrate individual leadership and achievement.
- State standards do not collectively address the breadth and depth of women's history. Rather, standards address a minority of topics and groups.
- Standards over emphasize women in their domestic roles without placing women's activities in broader economic, cultural, or political contexts.
- A small number of topics or eras that are commonly associated with being women-centric are emphasized, such as the Progressive Era and Woman Suffrage/Voting Rights.
- The presentation of women within standards does not reflect current scholarship.
- Standards do not reflect current trends or ideals in girls' education. While there is an increasing public interest in motivating girls to embrace science, technology, engineering, and mathematics, social studies standards provide few historic examples of women or their achievements in these fields.

The Takeaway

This result of this project is a *data set* of women and topics within US history standards. The state standards are not *women's history* as understood by academic historians. Women's history studies historical events, topics, people, and subjects from a woman's perspective. It understands that culture affects experience and that women's historical experiences differed from men's. Women's history contextualizes women within the social, political, legal, and cultural systems of their times. History that does not acknowledge women's situations as well as their activities and accomplishments is, by definition, not a full history. We found that women's topics are often an addendum to the main storyline. Women are frequently included in lists of marginalized groups as a reminder to teachers that when covering a broad topic, they should also include the experiences of *women* among others.

Now that we have identified the common women's topics in history standards, the National Women's History Museum will embark on the next phase of our curriculum project. Throughout the next year, staff will work with master educators, scholars, and public history experts to create a wealth of materials to support teachers and students. Our emphasis will be on the topics in national standards to ensure that teachers have high quality materials in specified topic areas. And we will further create materials that integrate women's historical experiences across the curriculum. Educators and parents will be able to examine any historical topic from a woman's perspective while meeting standards' learning objectives.

Call to Action

The current standards represent an opportunity for thoughtful dialog around women's history in K-12 public education. An opportunity exists for researchers to make more in-depth explorations of how women's history is presented in the US state standards. We hope that this report will inspire teachers, scholars, students, and parents to examine the ways in which women's historical experiences are presented in classrooms. We encourage all our stakeholders to advocate for the inclusion of women's history in standards, and therefore curriculum, now and into the future.

8

How to Make Room for Women in the History Curriculum

Margaret Smith Crocco

Margaret Smith Crocco is an educational historian, professor, and chairperson of the department of teacher education in the College of Education at Michigan State University. Her research focuses on gender and pedagogy.

Although the inclusion of women in history curricula in the United States has increased over the past several decades, educational historian Margaret Smith Crocco finds that it is often only tacked on as an afterthought or addendum to the history of men's accomplishments, which remains the centerpiece of the subject. Crocco proposes teaching women's history in "phases," which she outlines, to ensure that the curriculum is as inclusive as possible without sacrificing breadth in a survey course. She also asserts that this new curriculum would prevent women from being relegated to domestic and supporting roles in the study of history.

Women's history has come a considerable distance from its consolidation as a field of inquiry during the days of "second wave feminism" in the nineteen sixties.[1] At this time, Gerda Lerner wrote a dissertation that helped to revitalize the field established by Mary Beard earlier in the century. Lerner

Margaret Crocco, "Making Time for Women's History ... When Your Survey Course Is Already Filled to Overflowing," *Social Education* 61, No. 1 (January 1997), pp. 32–37. Reprinted by permission of the National Council for the Social Studies (www. socialstudies.org).

recalls that when she announced her intention of writing a dissertation on Sarah and Angelina Grimké to her doctoral committee at Columbia University, she was greeted by blank stares. Despite this reaction, she remembers thinking, "I want women's history to be part of every curriculum on every level, and I want people to be able to specialize and take Ph.D.'s in the subject and not have to say they are doing something else. I want women's history respected and legitimized in the historical profession."[2]

Lerner's vision has largely been realized at the university level. However, at the secondary level, my experience as a staff developer and teacher educator suggests that many present and future school teachers are still largely unfamiliar with the subject, and thus handicapped in incorporating women's history into their curricula. While primary and secondary level materials in women's history, and articles on how to infuse these resources into the curriculum, now exist,[3] it seems that many teachers still give women's history short shrift.

A number of factors explain this state of affairs. Teachers' lack of content background, the pressures for coverage in survey courses, and definitions of what's "important" based on what is included in standardized tests, have all limited the amount of attention given women's history in the schools. Even though women represent half the world's population, and in that sense have experienced half of human history, their stories are often marginalized if not omitted entirely when world or American history is taught in the nation's classrooms.

Moreover, the neglect of women's history persists despite the fact that many publishers feature "women's contributions" in their textbooks, if only by way of an occasional sidebar. This approach has often been disparaged as "add women and stir," and in truth, little mixing of women's history with the main events occurs when the subject is presented via sidebars. Such presentation may be preferable to women's absence from textbooks altogether; nevertheless, it suggests the degree to which the social studies curriculum has depicted women's stories as peripheral to the real story of political and economic history. Teachers whose own education has emphasized these traditional perspectives are often reluctant to address topics from social and women's history with which they are not familiar. Thus many factors collude to keep women on the margins.

Good reasons exist for making an effort at gender balancing the high school social studies curriculum. In this short essay, I will address the questions of why and how to include women's history at the secondary level in ways that underscore its significance without requiring that the teacher give up everything else he or she is obliged to cover.

Why Teach Women's History?

Curriculum theorists agree that creating and delivering curriculum is a normative process.[4] In essence, a curriculum represents truth and cultural significance for students. If women's lives (or those of non-elite men) get left out of the curriculum, students receive a message that these lives have been unimportant to history. If political and economic history crowd out social history, and by extension, women's history, then students get the message that childbearing and childrearing, subsistence agriculture, the building of a social order, and the care and maintenance of communities have had little significance over time. Only wars, political power, industrial and technological development, economic evolution and convulsion count in this scheme of history.

A second problem with an approach to history that makes women invisible is the incomplete understanding of the world that such treatment imparts. If male history gets substituted for all human history, the fallacy of this part-for-whole substitution falsifies the story of the past.[5] Since men's and women's experiences have been substantially different, collapsing women's history into men's history creates an inaccurate representation of the past. Men's story gets told; women's gets left out. Thus, not only do women's lives not count in the story of civilization, but men's lives "stand in" for women's lives, essentially rendering women invisible to history.

Of course, it should be noted that in traditional "great man" history, many men's lives get left out of history as well.[6] Traditional history features the "winners," those who have achieved political or military glory, great wealth, fame, or title. While the last two decades have witnessed a profound shift away from this elitist representation of the past at the university level, again my experiences suggest that the impact at the secondary level has been more limited. Even in settings where much attention is given to multicultural content, the attention to gender balancing this content suggested by scholars such as James Banks[7] often does not get priority.

Arguments for gender balancing can be made from the standpoint of both its truth value and the need to correct for the skewing that results when the curriculum reflects contributions only to public culture. A further rationale speaks more directly to the reality of the student sitting in the classroom. According to Emily Style,

"If the student is understood as occupying a dwelling of self, education needs to enable the student to look through window frames in order to see the realities of others and into mirrors in order to see her/his own reality reflected. Knowledge of both types of framing is basic to a balanced education which is committed to affirming the essential dialogue between the self and the world."[8]

Such an approach strikes the right note in its dual emphasis on curriculum as connection to students' lives as well as curriculum as conduit into the lives of others. The challenge lies in creating a "both/and" rather than an "either/or" curriculum. Depending on context, different teachers will surely calibrate their solutions to the "both/and" challenge differently; nevertheless the principle will remain the same. Both the stories of the powerful and the lives of women and others who are less powerful should find a place in the secondary social studies curriculum. This is true, in my view, whether the students represent the powerful or the dispossessed, women or men, Black, Latino, Asian or White, gay, lesbian or straight. The key is striking a balance.

Five Phases of Women's History

Incorporating materials about women into the standard survey course can be accomplished in a variety of ways.[9] In this essay, I have chosen to highlight Peggy McIntosh's approach. Each of her five "phases" in the treatment of women's history raises the ante in considering the assumptions and values that shape what gets taught. McIntosh begins with the question, "How would the discipline need to change to reflect the fact that half the world's population are women and have had, in one sense, half the world's experience?"

McIntosh stresses that her schema is not meant to represent a ladder-like progression in curriculum revision. The five phases were deliberately not labeled "levels," so as not to imply a hierarchical relationship between each one. She suggests that phase five curriculum has scarcely been imagined at this point in time; thus, its contours are the least well defined. Analogously, in James Banks' writing on multicultural education,[10] he posits evolution towards a transformative curriculum that culminates in social activism by students based on the material studied. Nel Noddings[11] has called for a rethinking of the social studies curriculum that derives from a more holistic approach to students' needs, one that considers both the private and public dimensions of their lives. These approaches may cast light on what McIntosh had in mind in sketching out the possibilities for phase five curriculum.

Overall, for the discipline of history, the shift from phase one to phase four involves a move from the question, "What did women do or produce that was important?," to the question, "How did past women live their lives?" For example, art historians or literary historians can substitute the question, "Did women paint or write anything good in the past?," with the questions, "What did women write?" and "How did women express themselves artistically?" Phase four work recognizes that the assessment of historical significance has been based on standards that reflect male experience and its normative framework. It critiques these postulates about historical significance by problematizing traditional standards and uncovering the male bias inherent in them.

McIntosh's framework will become clearer as we go through the phases and then develop one example. In phase one, the focus is on "greatness." Women are absent and their absence seems "natural." Phase two features the women who are "not like other women." These women represent the exceptions that prove the rule that women are incapable of the highest levels of achievement.

Phase three moves toward "systemic seeing." The focus of historical understanding shifts to a split screen analysis: individuals as part of groups and the systems that oppress them. The study of women's history now recognizes that cultural systems support, privilege, or thwart individuals, and this eventuality correlates highly with the individual's group identity. Freedom and agency are not denied; however, the social context is viewed as highly determinative of the scope for individual action and the possibilities for public recognition.

In phase three, for the first time, a feminist consciousness emerges; patriarchy is understood as having benefited a small set of "winners" while oppressing most women. Because of this awareness, the emotional tone of phase three curriculum shifts towards anger. Phase three highlights women who have challenged patriarchy: labor organizers, suffragist and equal rights leaders, "the new woman" of the twenties and "the women's libber" of the seventies, advocates of women's reproductive rights, and sexual harassment victims.

As curriculum re-visioning moves into phase four, a sea change in the normative framework results in a major reconsideration of what gets taught. Women's lives become history. Indeed, all of ordinary life finds itself part of history. The unrecognized and unrewarded women and men of all races, classes, and ethnicities who have participated in the behind-the-scenes work that sustains the pinnacle achievements of a few famous men find acknowledgment in the curriculum. Because of its emphasis on multiple perspectives, phase four women's history avoids the pitfalls of seeing women's history monoculturally, emphasizing an understanding that the racial, ethnic, and class differences of women's history as well as men's must be addressed by the curriculum.[12] Women's and men's multiple realities, multiple perspectives and multiple identities have shaped history in concert.

The Antebellum Period in Four Phases

Analyzing approaches to the antebellum period in the American history survey course can show how this process of inclusion works more concretely. In phase one, the teacher focuses exclusively on the national events leading from the Mexican War to the Civil War, emphasizing efforts in Congress to deal with manifest destiny and hold the nation together as tensions escalate over the spread of slavery. Politicians, states' rights, Congressional compromises, and manifest destiny define the contours of the curriculum.

In phase two, a teacher might add Dorothea Dix and her work to develop more humane modes of treating the mentally ill, and Harriet Beecher Stowe, called by Lincoln the "little lady who began the Civil War." Phase three history might add Elizabeth Cady Stanton, Lucretia Mott, and the Seneca Falls meeting that produced the "Declaration of Sentiments" on women's rights. So far, a few extra names, dates, and facts have been added to the curriculum, which may feel compressed but retains its structural emphasis derived from politics, economics, and military milestones.

Up to this point, the teacher has emphasized the contributions of forgotten women to the patriotic drama of American history. Because these approaches have not required reformulation of the traditional political and economic orientation, certain economies of scale apply. Women are no longer invisible; indeed, the idea has surfaced that women and men were not treated equally under past American political and economic arrangements.

In phase four, a teacher must tackle a more comprehensive reworking of the curriculum. Now the teacher needs to explain why the "Declaration of Sentiments" was such a radical document, that is, how women's lack of property rights, lack of access to an education, and inability to initiate divorce or maintain custody rights, contributed to the texture of women's lives. The class will also consider the content of different women's lives-on the Overland Trail and on the plantation, in the factories of the North, and among the Native American tribes of the West.

Juxtaposition of the diaries of Harriet Jacobs[13] and Mary Boykin Chestnut[14] can provide different perspectives on women's views of slavery: that of the slave and that of the mistress. Comparison of the life of a female slave[15] with that of a Lowell mill girl[16] can offer a lens on women's work outside the household and the varied meanings of "freedom" during this period. In both cases, such discussion, as McIntosh[17] notes, leads inevitably to treatment of Abraham Lincoln. However, if the unit begins with Lincoln, the student may never get to the voice of the slave, mistress, or mill worker. Phase four treatment of antebellum America also provides glimpses of women's involvement in the temperance and abolitionist movements, the harsh conditions of life in a sodhouse or in a Western mining town, and the disruptions in Native American life produced by westward expansion of the European Americans.

Clearly, phase four treatment of women's history requires compromise in the content covered. Perhaps less time will be given to covering the battles of the Mexican War or the Civil War; instead, emphasis will be placed on the causes, turning points, and outcomes of these conflicts. Letters, diaries, tracts, and novels written by women during the antebellum period—an outpouring which Nathaniel Hawthorne found vexing enough to complain that "those damned women scribblers" were outselling him—will add new dimensions to the understanding of the past.

In making these changes, however, fresh consideration of the conventional periodization found in textbooks will be necessary.

Now the question emerges: Are the years 1820 to 1860 best dealt with under the heading, "the antebellum period" (the political history rubric), or under the heading, "the age of reform" (the social history rubric)? Were these decades of reform or retrenchment for women? Is there only one perspective on this period, that of prelude to Civil War? In the lives of men and women between 1820 and 1860, what were the conditions that had the greatest long term cultural effect? These are some of the tough questions that teachers must face as they do phase four curriculum transformation.

Clearly, incorporating women's history into the secondary curriculum offers an instance of what Andy Hargreaves[18] calls the "intensification" of the teacher's role. While various national standards or state curriculum frameworks may call for greater inclusion of material on women and multiculturalism, the teacher's role as "curricular-instructional gatekeeper"[19] will only result in unwanted innovations being left outside the classroom door unless teachers feel some ownership of these changes.

It is important to keep in mind that only a minority of American youngsters attend college. A high school social studies curriculum that offers only a partial understanding of the past, that views history through a single lens, and that excludes women's stories, does a tremendous disservice to students whose education ends with high school. Like college graduates, they will inherit a world in which multiplicity and diversity define everyday reality. Those who have been schooled to one dimensional and overly generalized ways of thinking will find themselves at a serious disadvantage.

Notes

1. J. DeHart, "The New Feminism and the Dynamics of Social Change" in L. Kerber and J. DeHart, eds., *Women's America* (New York: Oxford University Press, 1995).

2. Gerda Lerner, *The Majority Finds Its Past: Placing Women in History* (New York: Oxford University Press, 1979).

3. Margaret Crocco, "Women's History of the 1920's: A Look at Anzia Yezierska and Charlotte Perkins Gilman" in *Social Education* 59, 1 (1995a), 29–30; Id., "The Road to the Vote: Women, Suffrage, and the Public Sphere" in *Social Education* 59, 5 (1995b), 257–264; M. Tetrault, "Women, Gender and the Social Studies" in *Social Education* 51, 2 (1987), 167–205.

4. S. Thornton, Lecture in "The History of Social Studies" (New York: Teachers College, Columbia University, 1/1996).

5. E. Minnich, *Transforming Knowledge* (Philadelphia: Temple University Press, 1990).

6. A. Chapman, *Feminist Resources for Schools and Colleges: A Guide to Curricular Materials* (Old Westbury, NY: The Feminist Press, 1986); Margaret Crocco, *Listening for All Voices: Gender Balancing the School Curriculum* (Summit, NJ: Oak Knoll School, 1988); L. Kerber and J. DeHart, eds. *Women's America* (New York: Oxford University Press, 1995); Peggy McIntosh, "Interactive Phases of Curricular and Personal Re-vision with Regards to Race. Working Paper No. 219" (Wellesley, MA: Wellesley College Center for Research on Women, 1986); E. Minnich, *Transforming Knowledge;* J. Zinsser, *History and Feminism: A Glass Half Full* (New York: Twayne Publishers, 1993).

7. J. Banks, *An Introduction to Multicultural Education* (Needham Heights, MA: Allyn and Bacon, 1990).

8. Emily Style, "Curriculum as Window and Mirror" in *Listening for All Voices: Gender Balancing the School Curriculum* (Summit, NJ: Oak Knoll School, 1988).

9. Gerda Lerner, *The Majority Finds Its Past;* Peggy McIntosh, "Interactive Phases of Curricular Re-vision: A Feminist Perspective. Working Paper No. 124" (Wellesley, MA: Wellesley College Center for Research on Women, 1983); M. Tetrault, "Women, Gender and the Social Studies."

10. J. Banks, *An Introduction to Multicultural Education.*

11. N. Noddings, "Social Studies and Feminism" in *Theory and Research in Social Education* 20, 3 (1992), 230–241.

12. E. Spellman, *Inessential Woman: Problems of Exclusion in Feminist Thought* (Boston: Beacon Press, 1988).

13. J. Yellin, *Incidents in the Life of a Slave Girl: Written by Herself, Harriet A. Jacobs* (Cambridge, MA: Harvard University Press: 1987).

14. C. Woodward, *Mary Chestnut's Civil War* (New Haven: Yale University Press, 1981).

15. J. Jones, *Labor of Love: Labor of Sorrow* (Boston: University of Massachusetts, 1990).

16. T. Dublin, *Women at Work* (New York: Columbia University Press, 1979).

17. Peggy McIntosh, "Interactive Phases of Curricular and Personal Re-vision with Regards to Race."

18. Andy Hargreaves, *Changing Teachers, Changing Times* (New York: Teachers College Press, 1995).

19. S. Thornton, "Teacher as Curricular Instructional Gatekeeper" in James Shaver, ed., *Handbook of Research on Social Studies Teaching and Learning* (New York: Macmillan, 1991).

9

Male Privilege and the Preference for Male Children

Heidi Shin

Heidi Shin is a journalist for Public Radio International. Her work has been featured on National Geographic Television and PBS's To the Contrary.

In South Korea, as in many countries around the world, it has long been the norm to desire a son over a daughter—so much so that many couples aborted their unborn children if they discovered they were female. However, Heidi Shin's viewpoint indicates that the preference for male children might be dwindling, along with other laws and attitudes that perpetuate male privilege, at least in South Korea. Nonetheless, although this suggests progress in the quest for gender equality, there is still a significant amount of room for improvement.

In South Korea, there's a new saying: "To have two daughters wins you a gold medal." But this wasn't the case a single generation ago, when couples would go to great lengths to conceive a son. A country's reverence for boys has turned into a slight preference for girls.

My Korean aunt, who is nearly 80, remembers the day she gave birth to her fourth daughter. "I cried so much, I almost fainted," she says. "I couldn't believe I had another daughter. Four daughters."

"In South Korea, Parents Are Increasingly Saying, 'We Hope for a Girl,'" by Heidi Shin, Public Radio International, December 8, 2016. Reprinted by permission.

She continues, "I had to keep having children, because I thought I needed a son. It's the only reason I have four kids. Not because I wanted four kids." There was immense pressure from her own mother, my grandmother, to give birth to an heir to the family.

Traditionally, Korea has been a Confucian society, which meant that sons inherited most of the property and carried on the family name. So in my aunt's generation, there are plenty of families with multiple daughters, and then finally a son.

But when ultrasound technology was introduced to South Korea in the late 1980s, suddenly far fewer girls were born.

"So many people aborted babies back then," my aunt says. "A few months in, when they could tell it was a girl, they'd get an abortion."

In the 1990s, there were 116 boys born for every 100 girls in South Korea. Gender imbalances at birth have also existed in other Asian countries like China and India. According to some estimates, there would have been 112 million more girls on the continent of Asia, had gender selective abortion and infanticide not existed.

In South Korea, the consequences were seen years later when the surviving boys grew up. There weren't enough women to marry in rural Korea—due to selected abortions and young, educated women moving to the big cities—so men turned to foreign mail order brides.

Now fast-forward 25 years to a new generation of parents, and many young Korean couples would prefer daughters. My cousin Seoyoung, who is a young mom, shares a new Korean saying with me: "There's really no use in having a son, because they just grow up to leave you, to take care of their wives."

In the past in Korean society, a son was required to carry out your family's ancestor worship. It's a set of elaborate Buddhist rituals in which the eldest son offers sacrificial foods to the family's deceased ancestors. Only men could make the offerings, while the women were required to prepare the food, often for days in advance.

But as Koreans are holding less tightly to Buddhist traditions—many have converted to Christianity—and people living longer, they're less concerned about being honored after death, and more concerned about being cared for while alive. As it turns out they say daughters are better for this than sons.

In the past, your oldest son and his wife would live with you until the end of life, but that's no longer the case. Sons are moving out when they get married, and parents are burdened with buying them new homes. This, while more elderly are living alone.

In contrast, young women like Seoyoung are moving closer to their aging parents. Because daycare options are limited, she depends on her mom for childcare. So now her parents have an adult daughter nearby to help them out with things like hospital visits and finances. In 2016, women have the means to do this, because girls are outperforming boys in school and getting better entry-level jobs.

Laws have changed too, allowing sons and daughters to inherit equally from their parents. When gender selective abortions peaked in the 1990s, the Korean government prohibited physicians from revealing a baby's gender in utero. Doctors who broke the rules had their licenses revoked and some were even sent to jail. The law was loosened later, and now obstetricians can share a baby's gender with patients in the second trimester, when an abortion is much less likely.

As a result, in 2016, the ratio of boys born in South Korea, compared to girls, is back on par with global averages. There are 105 boys born for every 100 girls each year.

The laws of nature dictate that a few more boys are born than girls, but overall, the numbers are almost even.

As for my cousin Seoyoung, she's grateful for her 2-year old daughter, and doesn't plan on having more. "I was so relieved that I didn't have to have a second baby," she shares. "I think I've gotten what I want."

Her friends with sons, though, they still talk about trying for a daughter, but they worry about the prospects of having another boy. According to Seoyoung, "That would be a disaster, they say."

My elderly aunt gathers with friends at a community center. They talk about the careers they wished they had had, and brag about the children they raised, both their sons and their daughters.

"Of course, I was disappointed then," my aunt shares. "But now I think, maybe I did a good job, having those girls. My daughters, they know my heart. So I'm not lonely."

But South Korea can still be a hard place for women, they admit. There's the immense pressure to conform to an unattainable standard of beauty, often through plastic surgery. Harassment in public is still common, and women aren't promoted at work in the same way as men.

I ask then, when it comes to grandchildren, do they prefer granddaughters to grandsons? Well, as it turns out, many young couples are choosing to have just one child or to be childfree. So most grandparents, they're grateful to have any grandchild at all.

10

The Health Impact of Male Privilege on Children

Seema Jayachandran and Rohini Pande

Seema Jayachandran is a professor of economics at Northwestern University. Rohini Pande is the Mohammed Kamal Professor of Public Policy at the Kennedy School of Government at Harvard University.

Through examining malnutrition rates among Indian and Sub-Saharan African children, it becomes clear that the advantages men experience in society can even extend to their health. The data discussed in this viewpoint indicates that girls in India experience higher rates of malnutrition than boys and their Sub-Saharan African counterparts, which is likely due to the societal preference for boys and the desire to have male heirs common to Indian society. As a result of the disadvantages faced by girls even before birth, the authors suggest that policies must be put in place to control and counteract son preference and the impact it has on health.

I ndian children are more likely to be malnourished than their counterparts in Sub-Saharan Africa, despite higher standards of living. This column uses data on child height—an anthropometric measure of net nutrition—from Africa and India to explore how parental gender preferences affect the likelihood of children being malnourished. Indian firstborn sons are found to have a height

"Son Preference Drives India's High Child Malnutrition Rates," by Seema Jayachandran and Rohini Pande, VoxEU, May 5, 2015. Reprinted by permission.

advantage over African firstborn sons, and the height disadvantage appears first in second-born children, increasing for subsequent births. This suggests that a preference for a healthy male heir influences fertility decisions and how parents allocate resources between their children.

It has long puzzled researchers that when you look at child height—the best anthropometric measure of net nutrition—the average child born in India is more likely to be stunted than her counterpart in Sub-Saharan Africa, even though her mother is more likely to survive her birth, and her parents are probably richer and more educated. In 2005, 40% of Indian children under the age of five remained stunted. Thus, despite a GDP per capita that is higher than over 60 countries, India has the fifth-highest stunting rate in the world.

Ramalingaswami et al dubbed this apparent contradiction "The South Asian enigma," and explanations offered since have included South Asia's breastfeeding and weaning conventions, its use of well water, its poorer treatment of women, and health problems associated with open defecation—which is more widespread in India than Africa and can cause children to suffer malnutrition even when they are well fed.

Yet these explanations fail to account for one important fact—Indian firstborns are taller than African firstborns. In a working paper, we analyse data on over 174,000 children from 25 Sub-Saharan African countries and India, drawn from recent Demographic and Health Surveys (DHS), and reveal that the Indian height disadvantage emerges with the second child and then increases with birth order. We propose that a preference for eldest sons in India (encompassing both a desire to have at least one son and for the eldest son to be healthy) leads families to dramatically reduce resources devoted to mothers and children over successive pregnancies, and that this drives the country's high malnutrition rates.

The evidence for this comes by comparing the height of children of different birth orders in India and Africa. The Indian height disadvantage appears for second-born children and increases for third and higher order births, at which point Indian children have a mean height-for-age lower than that of African children by 0.3 standard deviations of the worldwide distribution. The data shows this in terms of the stunting rate, using the World Health Organization's definition of having child height-for-age that is 2 standard deviations or more below the worldwide reference population median for one's gender and age in months. We see the same pattern—a much steeper birth order gradient in child height in India than in Africa—when looking only at children within the same family. Thus, the effect cannot arise from wealth or other differences in background of smaller versus larger families.

We also look at an array of health inputs—prenatal and postnatal check-ups, iron supplements, vaccinations—and as with height, we observe a steeper drop-off with birth order in India than Africa. The same holds true for children's blood haemoglobin levels.

Boys over Girls

While Indian children of both genders exhibit a sharper drop-off in height relative to African children, it is only among boys that we observe the advantage in height for Indian firstborns. Consistent with this fact, averaged across birth orders, the Indian height deficit only holds among girls. This suggests that prenatal investments are made in the form of nutrition and medical care as long as the parents believe the child might be a boy. When a girl's gender is revealed at birth, these investments drop off, and so does the height advantage she might have built up in the womb.

Furthermore, eldest son preference will generate the observed birth order gradient among boys simply because a lower birth order son is more likely to be the family's first son. Consistent with this argument, a son born at birth order 2 is taller in India than Africa if and only if he is the family's eldest son.

These patterns suggest that the prevalence of malnutrition in India is not an artefact of using child height to measure malnutrition, in which case low child height in India would simply reflect genetics. Genotypes do not vary with birth order or siblings' gender, so a genetic predisposition to be short would not cause the effects that we see. Other health- and environment-related factors that distinguish India from Africa such as India's worse maternal health and worse sanitation are potentially important in explaining the shortfall in height that is common across all Indian children but fail to account for the observed birth order patterns. Finally, the reason Indian later-borns are so malnourished cannot be that family income declines over the lifecycle in India relative to Africa. We find that it is only among pregnant women that women's health and nutrition in India and Africa have different time profiles; Indian women do relatively worse as family size grows, but only when they are pregnant, whereas declines in family income would be evident even when women are not pregnant.

It appears that families allocate inordinate resources—nutritious foods, iron supplements, tetanus shots and prenatal check-ups—to a pregnant woman as long as there is a possibility that she is carrying the family's firstborn son. Once a male heir is born, prenatal investments drop off.

Sibling Rivalry, but with a Prospective Sibling

Among girls, eldest son preference generates a birth order gradient through a more subtle mechanism, namely fertility stopping rules. Indian parents who start off only having daughters are likely to keep trying for a son, and in the process exceed the number of children they would otherwise have desired. Household resources dwindle and a later pregnancy is less well-resourced. If the later pregnancy yields yet another daughter, then she can receive even fewer resources than her older sisters because her parents have revised their fertility plans to keep trying for a son. Consistent with this, the India-Africa height gap is particularly large for daughters who only have girls as elder siblings.

Economists are familiar with the notion of "sibling rivalry," according to which siblings compete for household resources and girls who do not have a brother will show improved outcomes.

However, the pattern we observe stands in contrast to that prediction—in a household with only daughters, these girls will not benefit from being brother-less because their parents are keeping back resources as they keep trying for a male heir.

Religious and Regional Differences

When we leave aside comparisons with Africa to focus on patterns within India, we find more evidence supporting our interpretation that eldest son preference drives the country's high malnutrition rates. First, the height gradient is absent in Kerala, an Indian state with strong matrilineal traditions. Second, on average, Hindu children are taller than Muslim children, but not by the amount one would expect given Hindus' higher income. The data compares stunting rates between Indian Hindus and Muslims over birth order, and shows that Hindu firstborns are markedly taller than Muslim firstborns. It appears that Hindu parents seem to invest so little in their later-born children's health that, overall, they only show modest overall height advantage. For third and subsequent births, Hindu children fare worse than Muslim children in terms of height.

The difference may be due to religious as well as cultural norms. Hinduism prescribes a patrilocal and patrilineal kinship system—meaning, ageing parents live with their son, typically the eldest, and bequeath property to him. Also, Hindu religious texts stipulate that only a male heir perform certain post-death rituals, such as lighting the funeral pyre, taking the ashes to the Ganges River, and organising death anniversary ceremonies.

One might expect these household inequalities to reduce as India develops. The hope is that with greater financial resources, all children might be well nourished enough to achieve their height potential. However, when we compare households by wealth, the Indian birth order gradient in height is actually relatively larger among wealthier households. This echoes other forms of gender inequality that resist vanishing with development in South Asia as they do in other parts of the world. Richer and more educated

Indian women are less likely to work, and richer families are more likely to practice sex-selective abortion. Indeed, the problem of malnutrition already seems resistant to the forces of development—between 1992 and 2005 India's economic growth exceeded 6% per year, yet stunting declined by just 1.3% annually.

The beneficial forces of prosperity are strong, but social and religious norms may well be stronger. Unless policies are put in place to counteract the social and economic forces that support son preference, Indian families may continue to have more children than their ideal number, and Indian daughters may continue to receive less than their fair share.

11

What Are Microaggressions?

Alex Fradera

Alex Fradera is a psychologist and writer who focuses on organizational psychology and psychometrics.

Alex Fradera's viewpoint provides an overview of recent studies that complicate our understanding of microaggressions. Currently, microaggressions are defined as actions—intentional or unintentional, verbal or behavioral—that perpetuate the stereotypes of marginalized people. However, Fradera argues, when we remove the concept of power from the definition, microaggressions could be considered a larger sociological phenomenon that affects groups regardless of their level of privilege. While traditionally it has been considered an effect of privilege, Fradera suggests it is a more widespread phenomenon.

Microaggressions are seemingly innocuous words or behaviour that supposedly communicate a bias toward minority groups, such as asking Asian Americans where they are from, implying that they are not really part of the USA. According to advocates of the usefulness of the concept, microaggressions cause real harm, even if unintended by the perpetrator. However, the theoretical and evidential support for the concept of microaggressions is far from clear, as detailed in Scott Lilienfeld's recent thorough critique, which recommended the term be revised or at least re-examined. Now, Craig Harper, a psychologist at Nottingham Trent

"New Findings Pose More Problems for the Embattled Concept of the Microaggression," by Alex Fradera, The British Psychological Society, January 18, 2018. Reprinted by permission.

University, has published a study as a pre-print online at PsyArXiv that, he argues, reveals a further key problem with the concept of the microaggression.

As it's usually defined, a microaggression only counts as such when a *majority* group member commits an act that a *minority* group member perceives as a slight. The term was coined to account for slights against Black people, and has since expanded to other groups. On his *Psychology Today* blog, Derald Sue at Columbia University, one of the originators of the microaggression concept, states that microaggressions are "everyday verbal, nonverbal, and environmental slights, snubs, or insults, whether intentional or unintentional, that … target persons based solely upon their marginalized group membership." For his new study, Craig Harper's aim was to examine whether it's true that the experience of "being microaggressed at" really does only flow in one direction.

Harper recruited around 400 US participants online and split them into three groups according to their political beliefs: conservative, liberal, or moderate. They also answered questions about their pride in belonging to their political grouping.

The participants then read six fictional scenarios in which a professor made a contentious claim to his students. For example, in one, a male professor explained that the reason women are under-represented in certain professions is entirely due to their personal choice. A female student then responded in a frustrated manner, but was told by the professor to calm down and that this was not a place for "policy agendas." This is a fairly typical example of what the literature considers a microaggression.

Crucially, the scenarios were balanced so only half the microaggressions targeted people who would normally be seen as victims: women, Black people, and liberals. The other three scenarios kept the topics (such as educational attainment and political diversity), but switched the social identities of the perpetrator and victim. For example, in one case, a female professor justified lower rates of men in certain professions and then showed impatience towards a male student who complained.

After reading each scenario, the participants said whether they thought the student was right to feel insulted or had been overly sensitive. They also said whether they thought the professor was bigoted.

Unsurprisingly perhaps, the students' own political orientation shaped their response. Harper found that political liberals judged the fictional professors more harshly when they targeted racial minorities, women and those on the political left, compared to other targets. The students with more conservative leanings were less bothered by the scenario content overall, but showed the opposite pattern, being more critical when majorities, men and conservatives were targeted.

Harper says this is important because it shows, contrary to the conventional definition of the microaggression concept, that microaggressions aren't only experienced by those who fall into certain minority political categories. Instead it seems that anyone who thinks their in-group has been slighted by an out-group member may feel as if they've been "microaggressed."

Possibly relevant to one's sensitivity to potential microaggressions, according to Harper, is the concept of "collective narcissism"—how much we believe in the superiority of our in-group (typified by agreement with statements like "If people with my political views had a major say in the world, the world would be a much better place"). Based on the participants' ratings of their pride in their political in-group, there wasn't any evidence this factor mattered for the liberal groups' perception of microaggressions. For some of the conservative participants, however, it was those showing more collective narcissism who showed greater sensitivity to slighted right-wing targets.

This finding for collective narcissism is tentative at this stage. In fact, Harper's paper has not yet been peer reviewed and there may be further interpretations of the results that Harper hasn't considered. But it seems clear that once you are willing to put aside the lens of power to understand microaggressions, you can study the concept like other forms of motivated social cognition we understand quite well, such as, Harper says, the tendency "to shun or discredit those with whom we are ideologically opposed." These new findings suggest that those who argue microaggressions are a societal concern specifically afflicting minorities may have to recognise that other interest groups—especially in spaces that lean left, not right, like most universities—will have a claim to play the same game.

12

The Relationship Between Microaggressions and Victimhood Culture

Ronald Bailey

Ronald Bailey is a correspondent for Reason *magazine. He writes a weekly science and technology column.*

After assessing the current literature on microaggressions, Ronald Bailey argues that the term itself may be a symptom of the rise of victimhood culture in America. As a society approaches social equality, Bailey says, smaller slights against individuals in marginalized communities will garner larger reactions, leading to more conflict. In this way, Bailey asserts that microaggressions stem not from privilege, but instead from how an individual chooses to react to a perceived offense.

In "Microaggression and Moral Cultures," the California State University, Los Angeles sociologist Bradley Campbell and the West Virginia University sociologist Jason Manning identify a "culture of victimhood" that they distinguish from the "honor cultures" and "dignity cultures" of the past. In a victimhood culture, they write, "individuals and groups display high sensitivity to slight, have a tendency to handle conflicts through complaints to third parties, and seek to cultivate an image of being victims who deserve assistance."

"Victimhood Culture in America: Beyond Honor and Dignity," by Ronald Bailey, Reason. com and *Reason* magazine, September 11, 2015. Reprinted by permission.

Insightfully complementing their analysis is a new study by the St. Lawrence University economist Steven Horwitz, titled "Cooperation Over Coercion: The Importance of Unsupervised Childhood Play for Democracy and Liberalism." Horwitz makes the case that overprotective childrearing is undermining the "ability to engage in group problem solving and settle disputes without the intervention of outsiders," a capacity he calls "a key part of the liberal order." In other words, both studies find that Americans increasingly want and expect adult supervision.

Campbell and Manning begin by probing the rise of the "microaggression" phenomenon on university campuses. As defined by the Columbia diversity training specialist Derald Wing Sue, microaggressions are "brief and commonplace daily verbal, behavioral, and environmental indignities, whether intentional or unintentional, that communicate hostile, derogatory, or negative racial, gender, and sexual orientation, and religious slights and insults to the target person or group." Microaggressions include asking an Asian American where he or she was born, complimenting a Latino on speaking English well, or asserting that "America is the land of opportunity." In general, microaggressions are seen as instances of a larger narrative of structural inequalities. "Conduct is offensive because it perpetuates or increases the domination of some persons and groups by others," Campbell and Manning observe.

The authors argue that people seek the moral status of victim in situations where social stratification is low, cultural diversity is high, and authorities are referees. These three conditions pervade the modern American university, so it not surprising that the microaggression victimhood phenomenon is most intense in academia. Google Trends finds that headlines featuring microaggression started a steep rise in 2012.

As social status becomes more equal, they argue, people become more sensitive to any slights perceived as aiming to increase the level of inequality in a relationship. In addition, as cultural diversity increases, any attempts seen as trying to reduce it or diminish its importance are deemed as a morally deviant form of domination. As the New York University moral psychologist Jonathan Haidt has astutely observed, "As progress is made toward a more equal and humane society, it takes a smaller and smaller offense to trigger a high level of outrage. The goalposts shift, allowing participants to maintain a constant level of anger and constant level of perceived victimization."

Those experiencing what they think are microaggressions seek third-party redress of their grievances by assuming the pose of victim. "People portray themselves as oppressed by the powerful—as damaged, disadvantaged, and needy," write Campbell and Manning. The process heralds the emergence of a culture of victimhood that is distinct from earlier honor and dignity cultures. This is nothing less than demoralizing and polarizing.

In honor cultures, men maintain their honor by responding to insults, slights, and violations of rights by self-help violence. "Cultures of honor tend to arise in places where legal authority is weak or non-existent, and where a reputation for toughness is perhaps the only effective deterrent against predation or attack," write Campbell and Manning. They note that honor cultures still exist in the Arab world and among street gangs in Western societies.

During the 19th century, most Western societies began the moral transition toward dignity cultures in which all citizens are legally endowed with equal rights. Dignity does not depend upon reputation but exists as unalienable rights that do not depend on what other people think of one's bravery. Having a thick skin and shrugging off slights become virtues because they help maintain social peace. The aphorism that "sticks and stones may break my bones, but words will never hurt me," is practically the motto of dignity cultures.

Of course, serious conflicts cannot always be resolved privately. In dignity cultures persons, property, and rights are then defended as a last resort by recourse to third parties, such as courts and police, that if necessary wield violence on their behalf. Still, dignity cultures practice tolerance and are much more peaceful than honor cultures.

Horwitz is all about defending the culture of dignity. He points out that daily social interaction is full [of] annoying or obnoxious small-scale behavior such as failing to refill the copier, taking [someone] else's parking space, or hearing a tasteless joke. "When one seriously considers all the moments in a typical day that have potential for conflict that get resolved through conversation and negotiation, or just plain tolerance, it is actually somewhat astounding how smooth social life is," Horwitz observes. In fact, the vast majority of conflicts in modern Western societies are resolved without recourse to external authorities or direct coercion.

Horwitz makes a strong case that unsupervised and unstructured play among children teaches them private, noncoercive ways to resolve conflicts and generate cooperation, lessons that are very important to how they conduct themselves when they become adults. Supervised play, by contrast, trains children to expect adults to step in to adjudicate disputes and apply coercion. Horwitz fears this is flipping the social default setting from "figure out how to solve this conflict on your own" to "invoke force and/or third parties whenever conflict arises." He suggests that the recent upsurge in conflicts around sexual consent on campus may arise in part because so many young adults never acquired the social skills developed through unstructured play, such as "ensuring that all involved continue to consent to the rules and to the game being played."

Like Campbell and Manning, Horwitz notes that Americans are turning increasingly to third-party coercion to resolve what would in earlier days have been considered minor conflicts. He worries that without "the skills necessary to solve conflicts cooperatively, it is not hard to imagine that people will quickly turn either to external authorities like the state to resolve them, or would demand an exhaustive list of explicit rules" as to what constitutes permissible conduct. His concern mirrors that of Alexis de Tocqueville who in *Democracy in America* (1835) prophesied that democracy would generate an "immense and tutelary power" whose authority is "absolute, minute, regular, provident, and mild. It would be like the authority of a parent if, like that authority, its object was to prepare men for manhood; but it seeks, on the contrary, to keep them in perpetual childhood." Ultimately, Horwitz fears that the result of ceding ever more power to state authorities to resolve conflicts "will be the destruction of liberalism and democracy."

A victimhood culture combines an honor culture's quickness to take offense with an overdependence on the coercive institutions that serve as a dignity culture's last resort. If Campbell, Manning, and Horwitz are right about the direction American society is taking, that's really terrible news. A victimhood culture will spawn social conflict, which in turn will produce an ever larger and more coercive government tasked with trying to suppress it.

13

Transgender Individuals and Privilege

Leela Ginelle

Leela Ginelle is an author and journalist. She has written the books Game Night: A Role-Play Novel *and* Trans-y.

This viewpoint was written in response to a New York Times *op-ed that critiqued the inclusion of transgender women (women who were assigned male at birth and now identify as female) in feminism. The original article argued that because transgender women have not had the cultural experience of being a woman from birth and struggled with sexism in the same way cis-women (women who were assigned female at birth and still identify as female) have, they cannot fully take part in womanhood or feminism. Leela Ginelle, however, argues that transgender women do not experience male privilege, and in fact undergo discrimination and prejudice specific to their own identities as transgender individuals.*

This Sunday, the *New York Times* ran an op-ed by feminist filmmaker and journalist Elinor Burkett, titled "What Makes a Woman?" The piece voices Burkett's manifold complaints with the trans equality movement, focusing specifically on the ways trans women like Caitlyn Jenner express femininity and the manner in which trans visibility redefines the term "woman."

"Trans Women Are Women. Why Do We Have to Keep Saying This?" by Leela Ginelle, Bitch Media, June 9, 2015. Reprinted by permission of Bitch Media.

For trans women, Burkett's arguments are, sadly, nothing new. But with the recent explosion of trans visibility in mainstream culture, it feels important to offer a response.

Second-wave feminist thought was largely "trans exclusionary," meaning its members often expressed a refusal to see trans women as women. In the 1970s and 1980s, Gloria Steinem, Germaine Greer, Janice Raymond, and others held that trans women were aberrant and did not belong in the women's movement. Since then, some prominent feminists—including Steinem—have publicly changed their stances after hearing from trans people. But at the time, the main argument against recognizing the identities of trans women was two-fold and sometimes contradictory: Being a woman is a cultural experience and therefore only belongs to people raised from birth as girls, as cis women are. At the same time, the argument goes, trans women who would present as women using the trappings of traditional femininity—like dresses or Jenner's sexy corset—were holding back the movement's goal to get rid of the idea that being a woman required being traditionally feminine.

With cultural acceptance for the trans community rising, women such as Burkett—cis women accustomed to defining womanhood on their own terms—find themselves befuddled and aggrieved by notions of womanhood becoming even broader.

Burkett argues that "people who haven't lived their whole lives as women" shouldn't get to define what being a woman means. She writes:

> *"They haven't traveled through the world as women and been shaped by all that this entails. They haven't suffered through business meetings with men talking to their breasts or woken up after sex terrified they'd forgotten to take their birth control pills the day before. They haven't had to cope with the onset of their periods in the middle of a crowded subway, the humiliation of discovering that their male work partners' checks were far larger than theirs, or the fear of being too weak to ward off rapists."*

This is classic transphobia: a cis person believing their gender identity allows them to define "true" gender identities. It's saying: I have a uterus, and—despite you and all of your forms of hard-won legal ID saying you're female—I make the rules. As Burkett notes, though, the rules have changed. And she's upset by it.

Another trope among second-wave feminists' right to exclude trans women is the notion of residual "male privilege." Burkett employs that in her article, as well. Shortly after offering menstruation as the true mark of womanhood, she shifts gears and argues for acculturation. "Ms. Jenner's experience included a hefty dose of male privilege few women could possibly imagine," she writes, citing Jenner's athletic success, earning potential, and safety while walking at night as evidence.

To someone who saw trans women as men and had no understanding of—or empathy for—trans experiences, this might sound persuasive. However, this is not how trans women experience their forced misgendering. For many, many trans people, it is not all high wages and safe walks home at night. Instead, trans people face high rates of assault and can legally be fired for their gender identity in most states. In her interview with Diane Sawyer, Caitlyn Jenner offered an achingly honest account of the dysphoria and isolation she suffered as a closeted trans girl and woman, one with which I could identify.

For me, the experience of being a forcibly acculturated male involved my gender being misassigned at birth, years before it actually emerged. When I asserted my identity at the age of three, I was bullied and harassed until I disavowed it, learning to police my behavior and eliminate any femininity from my expression. I entered a world as a child that contained zero trans representation. Like a character in some dystopic novel, my identity was a frightening, shameful secret, and puberty was a confusing trauma. Any privilege I might have accrued feels well mitigated by the terror and self-loathing that defined my early life.

The idea of trans women's theoretical "male privilege" becomes even more distasteful when one considers trans women like Islan Nettles, and those like her, who are murdered simply because of her gender identity, or trans feminine youth like Leelah Alcorn, who take their lives because they can't imagine a future for themselves in a transmisogynist world.

Because women like Burkett do not see trans women as women, they tend to view our gender expressions to be mockeries of womanhood. Though they've worked throughout their lives to free women from sexist scrutiny, they freely scrutinize and ridicule the appearance of women like Caitlyn Jenner.

With derision, she describes Jenner's appearance in *Vanity Fair*, cataloging her "cleavage-boosting corset, sultry poses, (and) thick mascara." Were anyone to critique a cis woman this way, one imagines Burkett would take umbrage. Likewise, were one to extrapolate from a few photos that this was the subject's "idea of a woman," as Burkett does here with Jenner, one would think any feminist would take offense. Burkett seems to see trans women as interlopers or squatters in the land of femaledom. In a particularly offensive passage, she likens a trans woman to a young man who dies his skin and "crochets his hair into twists" and "expects to be embraced by the black community."

The clear theme of Burkett's article is that she does not wish to see gender redefined from the way she and her generation would have it set. In the article's second half, she offers a lengthy recitation of what might be called "occasions in which trans activists have argued for inclusive language," a list familiar to readers of Michelle Goldberg's articles on the issue. In observing recent requests by queer and trans people and their allies that abortion not be defined by vaginas, that *The Vagina Monologues* not be performed because of its exclusionary of trans identities, and that the term "sisterhood" be replaced by "siblinghood" at women's colleges, Burkett detects the definition of woman changing in a way that she thinks is misguided.

On the one hand, one can sympathize with how she feels, given that she and her cohorts worked hard to advance women's rights. Burkett clearly feels a stake in women's advancement and I respect that and the hard work she channeled into gaining gender equality years before I was born. On the other hand, though, if the feminists of a generation ago had not actively excluded transgender women, we wouldn't have to make as much of a ruckus today.

Throughout Burkett's life, trans women have lived largely on the margins of society (or in the closet) without rights or protections. Rather than see us as equals, many feminists of her generation insisted, as Burkett does still, on insulting and repudiating us. Our bodies are different, and, against our wills, so were our childhoods. From her perch, Burkett appoints herself to critique our appearance, language, and experience apparently without a lot of input from transgender people themselves.

Burkett writes that she wants to "rally behind the movement for transgender rights" and I believe her. Most people who believe in equality now do. For the communities who've been historically closest to them, meaning the LGBTQ and women's movements, supporting transgender rights today can mean having to face the ways they've excluded trans people and refused to see us as who we really are.

Supporting trans women means seeing them as equal to all other women. When you do this, then Caitlyn Jenner's self-expression is as valid as any other woman's. It means every trans woman's body is a woman's body and any definition of woman inherently includes trans women. If this is what Burkett means when she writes the trans movement is "demanding that women reconceptualize ourselves," then I suppose she's correct. It will be nice when people no longer see it as a "demand," though, and when people no longer ask, "What makes a woman?" and assuming the answer excludes transgender women.

14

Gay Men and Male Privilege

Rebecca Shaw

Rebecca Shaw is a writer whose work has been featured in the Guardian, Daily Life, *and* Junkee. *She also writes for the Australian television show* Tonightly with Tom Ballard.

Gay men occupy a complex position within the framework of male privilege. While they may face prejudice for their sexual orientation, Rebecca Shaw explains in her viewpoint, they hold onto their male privilege and speak over or discriminate against other marginalized groups, such as black, lesbian, or transgender women. This indicates that an individual can possess certain types of privilege, like those afforded to cis-gender men, while simultaneously lacking others, like the privilege that comes with being heterosexual.

I was recently sitting around with a group of female friends when, as it so often does in these settings, the subject of men's bad behaviour came up. On this night, everyone was sharing stories about men who have touched their bodies without consent, usually while the women were out on the town (do kids still say out on the town?). This is not surprising in itself—women sharing horror stories with each other about their difficult experiences with men is exceedingly common. What isn't *quite* as familiar is that on this

"Space Invaders: Why White Cis Gay Men Should Check Their Privilege," by Rebecca Shaw, Kill Your Darlings, March 17, 2016. Reprinted by permission.

night, it wasn't stories about heterosexual men and their behaviour we were discussing—it was stories about gay men.

In each of these stories, various women shared an analogous moment—upon (righteously) expressing shock or anger at the violation of their space, the man or men in question would generally play it off as a joke, or something that should not be upsetting—"it's okay because I'm gay." These men felt they had the right to debate her feelings and reaction in the situation because they are not sexually attracted to her—and therefore groping a woman's body is somehow excusable. Evidently, gay men can miss the point about women's autonomy just as spectacularly as heterosexual men.

It seems that this scenario occurs relatively often, but in the broader conversation about male violence against women, it is not widely discussed. It hasn't happened to me personally, but that may be because it's hard to get groped by strangers on a dance floor if you are in bed watching reality shows on your laptop. It's true that it is generally not gay men who are seriously injuring or assaulting or killing women. But that doesn't mean these types of actions are acceptable and should be ignored.

Sexism from gay men towards women often manifests in different ways to sexism from straight men. Gay men don't need or want women for sex, so the misogynists among them don't even have to bother presenting a façade of liking women. There are many gay men who have social circles that consist solely of other gay men. There are gay men who say vulgar and upsetting things about the body parts of women. We get it guys, you don't want to touch a vulva—it doesn't mean you need to compare it to fish at every opportunity. There are gay men who fetishise women of colour, ignoring them on a personal level but appropriating language and cultural touchstones and, in turn, perpetuating stereotypes. There are the gay men who would despise being thought of as someone's "sassy gay best friend," but who will claim that they have an "inner black woman" living inside them. Being part of a group that is itself stereotyped and fetishised, and sometimes treated as a toy to play with, it is confusing to comprehend so many men participating in these activities.

As is seemingly true for most articles written about heterosexual men, the obvious needs to be stated for certain people—Not All White Cis Gay Men (who are usually the people in question) are like this. Some of the privileges I'm talking about don't apply to gay men who are marginalised in other ways—through race, having a disability, being a sex worker, or operating in a system that discriminates against men with HIV. And not all WCGM (white cis gay men) go as far as groping women on dance floors. But still, among some, there does seem to be a lack of awareness of privilege.

I attended a conference last year that was full of diverse, progressive and smart young people. You'd typically expect white heterosexual men to be domineering in this kind of situation, based on, oh I don't know—every situation in all of history. However, I noticed that those (white heterosexual) men I encountered, broadly speaking, seemed aware and sensitive to the fact that they should do more listening than talking. The people who didn't get that same message? Some of the white cis gay men in attendance, who tended to automatically fill the space left by their heterosexual counterparts, going so far as to speak over women (including one guy pushing in front of a woman of colour to speak first, during a discussion about race).

And I get it. I am a white cis lesbian. I know that queer people like us are discriminated against. I know that we don't have marriage equality. I know that we are at higher risk of suicide, particularly young gay men. I know that I sometimes don't feel safe walking along the street as an openly lesbian woman, and that the threat of physical violence is even worse for gay men. I know that homophobia is painful, and that these men probably had to work to get to a place where they feel able to speak. But having those experiences doesn't entitle you to speak over other marginalised voices. It doesn't give you the right to treat women badly, or to dismiss lesbians or trans women or women of colour.

This amplification of WCGM voices to the detriment of others occurs everywhere, not just at conferences. Have a look at the people who often create or work at queer media (like websites or magazines). If you look at who is in charge, and who most of the editors and writers are, you will see it is still a field dominated by WCGM. If you look at who often runs marriage equality groups, and whose voices are most prominent in the debate, it is still often WCGM. And in these cases, they are not just speaking for themselves in a gay-male focused organisation—they've made themselves representatives for the entire LGBTQI community. They frequently do a good job, and they often try to include other members of the alphabet—but it is yet another system where certain types of people are placed in the power positions. And it is no coincidence that they're often white men.

In a country like Australia, white gay men are oppressed in certain ways by homophobia, but they also operate in a system that privileges men, including gay men, over women. It's a system that is hard for them to operate outside of, or to fight against, because it benefits them in multiple ways. But, some of my best friends are white cis gay men. This is precisely why I find it so perplexing when gay men act in sexist or misogynistic ways, and it's why I know they can do better. Certain groups of gay men have been attacked and bullied because they don't fulfil what the patriarchy says 'masculinity' should be. There is still a culture within the gay community of deriding 'feminine' characteristics, and an exulting of the 'masculine'.

Perhaps being brought up in a society that hates women so much it attacks men for displaying feminine characteristics is part of why some gay men remain oblivious to their privilege, and why they remain separated from women, both politically and socially. But this denigration of us all is the exact reason otherwise-privileged gay men should join forces with lesbians, and with other women, to work with us, rather than against us, in defeating the patriarchy.

15

Unconscious Bias and Its Role in Male Privilege

Laura Liswood

Laura Liswood is the Secretary-General of the Council of Women World Leaders.

In this viewpoint, Laura Liswood examines how unconscious bias enables male privilege to occur in the workplace. She defines "unconscious bias" as preferences and beliefs that we are not even aware we possess, which makes them particularly difficult to address. In the workplace, women are not granted the same informal mentoring that men are and are often perceived as being less naturally capable because of their gender. Men are also inclined to overestimate the percentage of women that work for a company and to believe their female colleagues receive an unfair advantage, which causes fewer women to be hired and promoted going forward.

The World Economic Forum estimates gender parity globally may now be over 170 years away. Previously they estimated an 80-year time, then it was 120 years. It keeps slowing down. The Forum's Annual Gender Gap Report shows slow progress and minimal change in many countries worldwide. What is causing this glacial pace of change, something the airline industry calls a "creeping delay"?

"Here's Why Gender Equality Is Taking So Long," by Laura Liswood, World Economic Forum, September 20, 2017. Reprinted by permission.

There are many headwinds that can lengthen the time required for desired systemic change, but there is one I'd like to address here, head on, and it's this: unconscious bias.

In general, there is a lack of awareness about who others are and what their capabilities and inherent qualities may be. In corporations, this often manifests as a culture that is unfriendly or unhelpful to women.

It's All About Power

What is unconscious bias? It can include anything from the preferences and perspectives we hold to the associations, roles and behaviours we carry out. A large part of it may be down to unconscious grievance and loss.

A "manifesto" written by a male Google employee this summer is a case in point. He posited that there are inherent psychological differences between men and women which lead to a disparity in how successful they are in the world of tech. It's clear that this man, and many like him, see diversity as eroding meritocracy and destroying the level playing field.

It is not my place to question whether Google was correct in firing him; he had his point to make. But I will say that whether he knows it or not, he is unconsciously finding selective arguments to resist change. He has something to lose.

The Google manifesto reflected this employee's belief that everyone lives in the same world as he does. But his is not a universal experience. He is unlikely to have been subject to systematic interruptions and the repeated questioning of his credentials or capabilities. He probably wasn't assumed to be incompetent until he proved otherwise, or excluded from informal mentoring or "bro" bonding. It's doubtful his comments were seen as aggressive rather than assertive, and that he was seldom acknowledged or taken seriously.

It's true the young engineer may have had some of this happen to him; but statistically, as a white male, he would not have experienced it at the same level or intensity as his female colleagues, nor felt its cumulative impact. He is unaware of the subtle advantages and perceived abilities "naturally" attributed to him. He may not truly grasp that for many women, their lack of success can be explained in part by the less-than-level playing field they work in. If it is made truly level, he will lose that subtle advantage he doesn't even see. The presence of capable women threatens the norms he has become used to.

When Equality Equals Loss

I believe there is a need to look closely at the loss and grievance that the dominant group feels when those from the non-dominant groups start to encroach on their societal position. In her book *Why So Slow*, Virginia Valerian found that while men can embrace the need for efforts that lead to fairness, such as equal pay, they have a much harder time with their own loss of centrality. This is about entitlement and holding a privileged place in the home, at work and in society. The loss of that privilege is a severe grievance.

For example, it is accurate to state that manufacturing jobs are diminishing and care jobs are in demand. It is quite another to have men accept new gender roles that they find emasculating. One survey focused in Middle Eastern and North African countries found that men harass women in public "to put them in their place." Much of the objection to change in gender roles is really about gender and power, not just about gender.

Joan C. Williams reflects on changing gender roles in her book *White Working Class: Overcoming Class Cluelessness in America*. She talks about "good" men and "real" men. The former are supportive, empathetic, collaborative. The latter are men who work in clearly identified masculine jobs, are assertive, take leadership at home and at work.

If we ask men to change their definitions of themselves it is not surprising that many will resist and find reasons to be critical of those they perceive as forcing this change upon them.

Geena Davis, at her eponymous media institute, has found that when a room's population is 20% women, men see 50%. When it is

30%, men feel it as 60%. The American Council on Education did a study asking teachers to call on boys and girls as best they could 50/50. After the experiment, the boys were asked how it felt. Their common response was: "The girls were getting all the attention." The boys (and men) feel a loss when equality is achieved. They have normalised overbalance.

As digital technology brings about massive global change, the World Economic Forum, which calls this shift the Fourth Industrial Revolution, is working to ready society for the upcoming disruptions. But for some, moving from a gendered position will feel like a loss, even though the shift may ironically reflect a more equal society.

16

Male Privilege Leads to Domestic and Public Acts of Violence

Jo Scott-Coe

Jo Scott-Coe is assistant department chair and an associate professor of English composition, literature, and creative writing at Riverside City College in California. She researches gender, sexuality, and violence and is the author of various nonfiction works, including the book MASS: A Sniper, a Father, and a Priest.

While mass killings tend to receive a large amount of media coverage, domestic violence against women generally does not. Jo Scott-Coe explains why misogynistic domestic violence deserves more attention through using the case of mass murderer Charles Whitman to examine the relationship between domestic and public violence and how the expectations and privileges of masculinity connect the two. In a society where men are allowed to judge and control women—a privilege that is enforced by the way the media depicts Whitman and his victims—violence against women can often go unacknowledged.

Repeated true-crime narratives tend to deflect serious examination of the misogynistic attitudes, abuse, and/or fatal violence that too frequently precede a public massacre. A reconsideration of surviving writings by Charles Whitman, the

1966 UT Austin sniper, alongside newly-discovered letters of his wife and second victim, Kathy Leissner, reveals how inflexible gender attitudes and judgments took a profoundly toxic and eventually fatal toll in private, long before Whitman's display of hyper-masculine force from atop a landmark tower.

Four years ago, in an essay titled "Shooting Sprees Start with Women," I explored how the private brutality that precedes violent spectacle is often buried by coverage of the public event. An accumulation of such stories—from Sandy Hook to Orlando, from Casper College to UCLA—still treats domestic death or wounding as an afterthought to more serious or offensive crimes.

As a result, those terrorized in private do not fully register on the compass of collective outrage, except as targets of direct or indirect blame for the public outcome. In 2015, Bill Maher argued on his show *Real Time* that young males commit mass killings because they simply can't "get laid," even though commercials depict women as ready and willing sexual objects (n. pag.). Maher didn't mention to his applauding audience that a significant percentage of these same men stalk, abuse, or kill women as a prelude to attacking strangers (Everytown 2–5). Furthermore, Maher's commentary unwittingly replicated the entitled misogynist "reasoning" often broadcast by the killers themselves (Schonfeld)— as in the cases of Marc Lepine (1989), George Hennard (1991), George Sodini (2009), and Elliot Rodger (2014).

One enduring example shows how ingrained our current script and its gendered erasures can be. Since 1966, writers, artists, and documentarians have retold the story of Charles Whitman's clock tower rampage at the University of Texas at Austin, which left nearly fifty people dead or wounded, including Whitman himself. Unlike most mass killers, he was married rather than single. But like many others, he murdered women at home—his mother, Margaret, and his wife, Kathleen—before shooting anyone else. And like many men who commit similar attacks, Whitman viewed women as objects both to desire and control.

It is important to examine how the UT Austin narrative—like so many others—diminishes, romanticizes, or sequesters domestic murder. I will argue that this repeating dynamic reflects something all too ordinary and self-implicating: fear and suspicion of women. Whitman's actions and personal writings must be understood within this context. Newly available primary documents finally make it possible to consider the perspective of his wife as well as her family.

Charles Whitman's 1966 Rampage

The UT rampage was not the first mass murder in American history, but it was the first televised shooting of its kind, and the sensational scale of Whitman's crimes generated media headlines across the country. For five decades, the story has been a subject for continued "true crime" exploration, inspiring made-for-TV style documentaries ranging from *The Deadly Tower* (1975) to *Deranged Killers: Charles Whitman* (2009). In 2016, the film, *Tower,* became the first theatrical release to document the experience of victims and survivors on the ground. Gary Lavergne's book, *A Sniper in the Tower* (1997), is considered the definitive synthesis of the case, so much so that Lavergne himself was the subject of a 2003 documentary for the History Channel's *True Crime Authors* miniseries ("Sniper in the Tower"). Story after story addresses Whitman's Eagle Scout achievement, his military training, drug use, fascination with guns, hatred of his father as well as his much-debated brain tumor (Ward). Limited attention has been paid to Whitman's attitudes about women and sex. Whitman's wife and mother are usually rendered through romantic/sensational re-enactments or minimalism/omission, all in service of "true crime" formula with its victims, heroes, and obvious villain. This repeated and recursive glossing suggests gendered habits of mind—both of authors and audiences—rather than direct intention or malice.

As a former Boy Scout and altar boy, as a handsome, white college student and former Marine, Whitman embodied the mid-century, postwar "All-American guy." Yet privileges of gender and race, bound with the motifs of American individualism, have cast Whitman as a "crazy, deranged individual who had suddenly gone completely berserk"—an exception to the rule (Special Report of the Grand Jury 1, par. 2). In his book, *Murder over a Girl,* Ken Corbett describes gendered inattention this way: "One of the ways that [boys] get to be boys is that they get to be invisible," meaning, in part, that classmates, colleagues, family, and friends "refuse to know what they knew" (151). In a similar vein, one of Whitman's peers recounted his pranks and other high-risk behaviors after the massacre with amusement and disbelief, saying: "If Charlie was a monster, then so are we all" (qtd. in Dugger 3).

There's yet another factor which has camouflaged Whitman's attitudes. In contrast with "lone-wolf" shooters who left behind over-the-top diatribes against women, Whitman's surviving letters and journals rely heavily on the language of idealization. Yet his attitudes are no less objectifying, despite his repetition of "love" and other flowery terms. Furthermore, his idealization divides women into simultaneous targets of worship and punishment (Madonna/whore), demonstrating what Julia Kristeva calls a "conjunction of opposites (courtliness and sadism)" (162–63). Rather than enacting an aberrant tangent, Whitman's first murders fulfilled—in the most extreme way—the code of mid-century American masculinity he had absorbed, practiced, and even struggled against, defining real men as dominant and powerful and real women as subordinate and submissive. The pattern normalizes victimization of women when individual men do not see themselves living up to the stereotype of their own gender: "The target must already be seen as legitimate [...] [M]asculinity may not be the experience of power. But it is the experience of *entitlement* to power" (Kimmel 181, 185).

Violence against woman can thus embody a primal, "restorative" strike to (re)assert masculine dominance, "returning [...] to the moment before that sense of vulnerability and dependency was felt" (Kimmel 177–78). Historian Gerda Lerner hypothesized that the awe-inspiring power of women was first venerated and then objectified, reflecting male dread, envy, and eventually ownership of the capacity to create and sustain life (45–53). In this way, Whitman's first murders can be understood as acts of self-ordination to "divine" male dominion over life and death—first in private, then from more than 300 feet above sidewalks and streets. It is no coincidence that his first target from the tower was a heavily pregnant woman, Claire Wilson, whose child was aborted in utero with his first bullet (Maitland). Confronted by repeated failures as a Marine, as a college engineering student, and as a husband, Whitman still felt entitled by a toxic residue of privileges he was born into as a white male Southerner. Storytelling that avoids (or "abjects") gender, sexuality, or race inadvertently re-inscribes that same toxic inheritance.

Depictions of Intimate Murder in the UT Austin Case

In addition to the investigative documents assembled by law enforcement agencies, a significant sample of Whitman's personal writing (from ages 15–25) was publicly preserved and is now housed in the Austin History Center. Documents in this archive include notebooks, a day planner from his first year of college, a diary, miscellaneous "inspirational" notes, and four letters he composed within hours of the shooting. This was the extent of the accessible record until 2015, when I was granted exclusive access to additional materials from the private collection maintained by his wife's eldest brother.

Over time certain documents—and parts of documents—have received more scrutiny than others. Whitman's simplistic references to "love" for his mother ("I loved that woman with all my heart") and his wife ("my most precious possession") have been inextricably bound to his justification for their murders. In the History Channel miniseries episode "Sniper in the Tower," Lavergne summarized a motive for the first two killings, sampling

Whitman's language from his typed letter the night before: "He probably killed them for the reason he said he killed them: to spare them the trauma and embarrassment of what he knew he was going to be doing later that morning." Lavergne, taking Whitman at his word, reserves "trauma and embarrassment" for the public acts "he was going to do later," inadvertently ennobling the private murders as tragic casualties of misguided valor or mistaken generosity (00:25:24–00:25:40).

We can see similar gaps of attention when it comes to the content of Whitman's writing in the scene where he murdered his mother. In the one-page letter he printed on yellow legal paper and left on his mother's body, he repeated twice that he had "relieved her of her suffering" at the hands of his father, to whom she had given "the best 25 years of her life." He portrayed himself as a divine agent, sending his mother to "heaven" after suffering from his father's abuse. But Whitman also added a grotesque verdict: "[My father] has chosen to treat her like a slut that you would bed down with, accept her favors, and then throw a pittance in return" ("To Whom It May Concern").

This statement is composed of two clauses—the ugly main clause and a long dependent clause—and only the very last phrase ("a pittance in return") has drawn serious attention. The language parallels two other final references to money and family: one, in a short note referring to forty dollars sent by his brother, Patrick; the other, a mention of his mother's "usual standard of living," hand-scrawled at the end of a typed letter found in his home. Understandably, like investigators after the crimes, Lavergne zeroed in closely on Whitman's accusation about his father as a withholding "provider":

> In an attempt to trivialize the area of life in which his father was clearly superior, Whitman again focused on what his father allegedly failed to provide for his mother [...] [His father] actually provided quite a good standard of living for his entire family, even after Margaret left Florida. There were allegations from Margaret's brothers, however, that [he] had cut off all financial support for

Margaret and Charles [...] only the day before [Charlie] decided
to become a mass murderer. (108)

While questions about economics are important, Whitman's
choice of words points us to something profound. Summing up
his father's treatment of his mother with a mixture of vulgarity
and delicacy communicates sexual shaming as well as a high-
stakes division between "mothers" (good women) and "sluts" (bad
women). Here, financial anxiety or blame cannot be isolated from
gender norms that divide women and assign heterosexual family
roles, protection, and ranks. Kathy's brother, Nelson Leissner,
informed me in an interview that Whitman's father called to brag
days before the shootings about his involvement with a woman
Kathy's age. (By November after the killings, his father married
again.) The question of divided resources would have been fraught
by any "threat" of a new sexual-familial relationship, particularly
with a younger woman who already had one child and another
on the way (Lomartire).

Such a "threat" would have mattered only to a young man
already deeply indoctrinated by masculine codes of competition,
female subjugation, and domestic purity. Some sons would
dismiss the sick hypocrisy of any father using sexual taunts to
pressure the abused mother to return. But this was an eldest son
who had married in a Catholic church on his parents' wedding
anniversary four years earlier, a son who was still not financially
independent and who feared that he might be sterile. Viewed
together, Whitman's ceremonious use of a brand new Bowie
knife and crushing his mother's wedding ring finger (Lavergne
102–03) gruesomely reference the attempted restoration of a
violated honor.

Blind spots in reconstructions of his wife's killing are even less
subtle. Kathy's murder is framed like a dark fairy tale, a convention
reinforced by her youth and beauty as well as her marriage bond
with her killer. Typical phrases are "killed in her sleep" (Garcia)
or "stabbed to death in her sleep" (Eagleman). Such passive
descriptions are shorthand for an approach used by Lavergne,

who recreated the scene entirely from Whitman's perspective. After describing his quiet approach to Kathy's bedside, his exposure of her nude body, and the "considerable strength" of "vicious thrusts" from his hunting knife, Lavergne concludes:

> *Given the size of the knife and the location of her wounds, Whitman probably hit her heart [...] Without struggle, Kathy died instantly [...] She most likely went from sleep to death without ever seeing her murderer. It was just as well. Whitman was right: she was as good a wife as anyone could hope. Her loyalty never wavered, even after physical assaults and mental anguish. She stayed with him until the very end.* (108)

This representation disallows entirely the possibility of Kathy's pain, terror, or physical resistance to an attack while at her most vulnerable—committed by the man with whom she had shared a bed. Ironically, Lavergne does imagine the possibility of Whitman's final homage to Kathy's body before he left the house, reinforcing the image of Kathy as an object of her husband's gaze: "No one will know if [he] looked at her one last time" (120). The result of the sequence is a perverse *aubade,* a violent lover's farewell. Kathy's qualities as "a good wife" (who "stays until the end") are also emphasized here, validated by the author's agreement with notes Whitman added above and below a journal entry from 1964: "I still mean it," he wrote. "My wife was a true person" (*Daily Record of CJ Whitman*).

Continued repetition of select declarations from Whitman, divorced from the context of his language and the dramatic irony of his violence, has unintentionally ratified them, perpetuating a wounding against the women and their families—and by extension, any women killed under similar circumstances. One enduring impact is to cast additional scrutiny of these scenes as unnecessary or unseemly, making narrative realism seem salacious in comparison to the common wisdom of the tale as repeated again and again. Another dangerous result is an overemphasis of the victimized party's character qualities as a necessary threshold for empathy from readers.

A Fractured Fairy Tale: Whitman as "Man"—Kathy as "Wife"

We can now read Whitman's attitudes by tracing them forward in select letters to Kathy beginning two months prior to their marriage. An even larger sample of her letters—both to Whitman and her own mother—provide insightful points of comparison, showing how she experienced his behavior as well as how she constructed her own responses. Whitman's posture of control is evident early on, prior even to the couple's official engagement, as in the first line of a letter referencing their dating relationship: "How's it feel to be tied down to the same fellow for 4 months, 1 day, 23 hours, and 35 minutes? I sure am glad I tied down that little dropper of mine." His fixation on a precise moment of "capture" and a third-person reference to Kathy as a "little dropper" together undermine his inquiry about her feelings. A sentence shortly afterwards supports this interpretation, as he critiques her latest letter: "Miss Leissner I have a bone to pick with you [...] if I want to read typewritten paper I can find plenty of it at the ROTC building" (12 June 1962, Select Letters).

Proprietary demands pepper Whitman's communication, and his sweetness or politeness always betrays an agenda. He treats Kathy's social connections as his own from the beginning: "Oh, ask Floyd [the Justice of the Peace] if he can sell me liability insurance. I am having some trouble here [...] Find out and let me know if he can insure me" (9 June 1962, Select Letters). His requests reinforce Kathy's expected menial or secretarial roles, such as sewing a patch on his karate outfit, taking care of floor mats for his new car, keeping track of clothing he left here or there, sending him a tinted photo of herself, cleaning their new apartment "the way she likes it," and wedding preparations—including a task traditionally performed by the groom: purchasing the wedding bands.

Whitman also casts himself as "expert" in odd ways, advising Kathy, for example, about getting a "premarital exam" because he'd seen an article in *Modern Bride*. (This after she has already informed him that she saw the family doctor.) He directs her to "get her teeth in good shape" because she won't be covered under his military dental policy, adding another comment that describes Kathy as a material property rather than a person: "Your dad's sure getting stung isn't he. Getting you ready to give to someone else" (24 July 1962, Select Letters).

By age twenty-one, Whitman was already heavily conforming to a paternalistic mode of relating to women, applying emotional pressure to get his way. His intention to marry simply emboldened and legitimized this "adult" posture. On occasions when Kathy's parents—particularly her father—raised doubts about a hasty wedding date, or whether Whitman should be allowed to stay overnight at their home, he pouts: "If I'm going to cause trouble I'd rather not come" (19 June 1962, Select Letters). The same letter includes an ultimatum to Kathy that pre-figures what he will write to his in-laws four years later: "I don't mean to hurt your Mom and Dad by taking you away, but if you marry me I'll expect you to go with me."

Letters written by Kathy and her mother reveal that there was a significant crisis within the first six months of marriage, due to what Kathy's mother called Whitman's "desire to dominate Kathy"—a desire revealed, in part, by his assertion that she "need[ed] to see a psychiatrist" because she had "changed" and was unhappy (qtd. in Scott-Coe "Listening"). Kathy's subsequent actions and letters indicate in various ways that while her husband continued to practice an ethos of control, she was testing her independence. Kathy initially left her family in February 1963 to withdraw from UT and join her husband on active duty in North Carolina, but after six months she also managed to get away from him and return to Texas, her family, and school when he was deployed to Cuba—despite disapproval from her in-laws as well as pressure from Whitman to have a baby (Scott-Coe "Listening").

Kathy's letters to Whitman during their separation (July 1963–Dec. 1964) provide many examples that demonstrate how she had internalized her husband's displeasure and adjusted to his preferences, even when it meant questioning her own judgment.

In a long letter after their first anniversary, she apologizes for making him mad and for complaining about not hearing from him, pledging not to "nag" him about his gambling. She also downplays a more intimate, and sad, concern: "Please don't think I still have that dumb notion of your only desiring me for sexual release" (Letters 27 Aug. 1963). However, the longer Kathy lives apart from Whitman, the more deeply her writing expresses desires for change in their relationship (Scott-Coe "But What Would *She* Say?"). She explores one of his insecurities at length in a letter dated 6 May 1964:

> [Y]ou think it's dependence but really that's the way it should have been when you first thought you were in-love with me [...] [I]t's going to be almost like getting to know each other again when you get out [...] [W]e are both going to have to realize that when we get back together and respect each other's new ideas. [n. pag.]

In another letter the following month, she worries that the "awful nice things" he said about her from a distance could be ominous:

> Honey, when your [sic] not with someone you love, it's awful easy to build them up to something they aren't and I'm afraid this may be what you're doing. I even got this impression when you were home on leave in May. You seemed a little dissatisfied with me in some ways and I really am the same girl you married. I may be unjustified in my fear but it could happen. (Letters, 13 June 1964)

Kathy's insight and her "fear"—framed cautiously around a specific recollection of his "dissatisfaction"—are poignantly attuned to the dangerous nature of the pedestal Whitman had placed her upon. In a different marriage, the couple's reunion in December 1964 might have brought Kathy's "new ideas" of "respect" and mutuality to fruition. Instead, Kathy's college diploma and professional status as a certificated science teacher would become threatening evidence to Whitman that she could thrive without him—and that she was capable of eluding his control.

The Problem of the Gender Pedestal

Whitman's use of a pedestal to elevate and to "measure" Kathy is documented in the diary he returned to after killing her. The entry dated 23 Feb. 1964, composed as he completed his sentence of hard labor following his special court martial, is often cited as proof of his affection. A more attentive reading, however, shows exactly how Whitman defined love, gender relations, and Kathy herself. The note he scrawled at the top—"I still mean it"—can only be interpreted favorably if we ignore the content of the entry he identified for posterity as important (Daily Record of CJ Whitman).

By framing our attention, Whitman sought to publicly perform his private ownership of Kathy; thus, his presentation enacts a pornographic aesthetic. Encompassing approximately four pages, the entry is one of the longest in a diary where the author left three-fourths of the pages blank. From the beginning, he writes of Kathy in terms that emphasize her use to him, twice repeating the phrase "most versatile" to describe her, and adding that she is "everything [he] want[s] in a wife," "the overall package," "the ultimate in a mistress," and "my most precious possession" (Daily Record). Furthermore, he includes cooking, sewing, and driving among her skills, as well the ability to learn quickly in sports or games.

Whitman's perspective is entirely reductive, with the first two pages itemizing Kathy's physical traits in comparison to "professional standards," for which—according to him—she comes up lacking: "not beautiful," "too short," not "a model's figure," "her knees and thighs are heavier than they should be" (Daily Record). He then selects certain parts as his to reshape ("we will be able to trim her legs down to the right proportions") and dismembers other body parts he approves of, which he isolates for competition "against any recognized bathing beauty." Ironically, he adds that his wife "is prone to feel inferior when she is in competition," as if his assessments had nothing to do with insecurities she felt about her body or her intelligence.

When it comes to their intimate life, Whitman refers to what he gets rather than gives, crediting himself for his wife's "sexual prowess [sic]," commenting that "her naivety [sic] in the first place is pretty responsible for her success at this venture [...] I have taught her how to please me, which she does so expertly" (Daily Record). He talks of sex in a depersonalized way—as a "venture" at which one "succeeds"—with Kathy merely being the winning contestant for his desire. He does not recount shared experiences or mutual discoveries.

Equally significant is how the entry explicitly positions Whitman as the superior male authority when assessing Kathy's character compared to other women's: "When I stand back and judge her," he writes, "it amazes me that such a young woman can possess such outstanding qualities" (Daily Record). He highlights her "common sense," an "important asset which so many women do not have." Predictably, his definition is entirely self-serving: "she detaches herself from her emotions and desires in spite of what she would like to do [...] quite extraordinary for her sex." Here, gender stereotypes substitute for specific women, and he counts himself lucky compared to other men, who "have to put up with nagging temperamental wenches who will not use common sense [...] to realize that what their husbands are doing is correct." Yet Whitman composed this entry while suffering serious military consequences for "incorrect" choices of his own, including the gambling that had worried his wife six months earlier. He seems vaguely aware that while he may be entitled to judge, he also falls short of his own standards. He writes that he hopes "to be worthy of" Kathy, and that "maybe someday [he]'ll be able to convince [her] of all the emotions and feelings." He also casts the possibility of his own failure "by society's standards" as a failure against Kathleen.

A scattering of other journal entries describes their relationship in zero-sum, high-stakes terms that do not bode well: "live and die as man and wife," "she is my whole life," and "without her, life would not be worth living." While in the brig awaiting his court martial, he expresses a morbid, clinical view of death: "I have thought very much about the concept 'death.' When it overtakes me someday I must remember to observe it closely and see if it is as I thought it would be" (Memoranda 13 Nov. 1963). He also links Kathy, fatefully, to moral responsibility and self-control, describing how thoughts of her "kept him from beating the hell" out of a military policeman who interrupted him on the phone (Memoranda 22 Jan. 1964), and later writing that "she is really what keeps me straight" (Memoranda 30 Jan. 1964). Interestingly, Whitman appropriates Kathy's moral authority as his own, emboldening more harsh judgments against others and allowing him another arena for competition: "Everyone I meet seems to look at me in awe when they realize I don't run around [...] [I]t ought to set some kind of record" (Daily Record of CJ Whitman 6 Mar.). When his boss questions him, Whitman reflects: "I couldn't convince him of how much Kathy means to me or how little sex with some whore means to me now that I have matured" (Daily Record of CJ Whitman 6 Mar.).

One long entry dated 13 March 1964 begins with how "Kathy would have been proud" of him for rebuffing sexual advances from another woman at Jazzland, a nightclub he frequented (and where he appeared to be employed in some capacity, likely as a bouncer): "I notice other women only to compare them with Kathy. They are all so far below her standards, she has them beat by miles" (Daily Record of CJ Whitman). At times, he transforms his standards to Kathy's, then projects his notions of "possession" onto her, writing: "Now that I am married, I feel as though I am her personal property and whenever another female touches me that she is violating my wife's property."

Letters from Kathy dated before and after this time (21 Feb., 23 Feb., and 28 May 1964) suggest that Whitman actively shared stories of past and present women while at the same time instructing Kathy "never to mention" them. He thus cast himself as a victim while also posing, sadistically, as judge for Kathy's reasonable insecurity.

By re-centering his final attention—and ours—on these paradoxes of possession and ever-elusive courtship, idealism and inadequacy, competition and failure, Whitman underscored how volatile these values could become. By identifying Kathy with the "angel in the house" from a long distance, he also made her vulnerable to gendered judgments, even gaslighting her, as "madwoman in the attic" upon their reunion. Worst of all, his pedestal made Kathy a primary target for elimination when his "common sense" ultimately dictated that violence was best.

New Artifact in an Old Story

One letter preserved by Kathy's family was written by Whitman and mailed to her parents the morning before the shootings on August 1. According to Nelson Leissner, it arrived the day of Kathy's funeral and burial and was kept private for nearly fifty years (Personal interview). In two pages composed on drafting paper, Whitman reprises similar themes and phrases in the letters left with his mother ("I was just causing her unnecessary suffering," "I believe she is in a happier place now," "I did Kathy a great favor"). His admissions of personal and gendered inadequacy are trapped in a loop of circular reasoning for "tak[ing] Kathy's life": "I am so ashamed that I could never support her as she deserved" or "I will always regret that I did not feel worthy of her" (Select Letters). He also discloses that he had been contemplating murder "for the last two days" and that he "tried to be as sweet as possible on this her last day." He then lists a childlike résumé of "sweet" activities as mitigating factors, including taking Kathy to lunch and seeing a movie during the break of her split shift at the phone company. He speaks on her behalf, stating that her "greatest fear in life was that we would be incapable of having children of our own."

As hideous as all this is, no parent would have been prepared for Whitman's turn in the second paragraph: "Tonight after she talked with you we shared a last interlude together, she has always been a fine lover. Then I tried my best to kill her as painlessly as possible, however, I have my doubts about how painless it was. She was a very strong girl" (Select Letters). The tangle of exhibitionism and romanticism—"shared" and "interlude"—makes the blasé transitions between sexual contact and brutality even more jarring. Whitman represents himself as final judge, including dehumanizing "compliments" and referring to Kathy as "girl" even in death.

It is difficult to face this document. However, it may help to remember that it was preserved rather than destroyed by her family, and that it witnesses the horror of Kathy's last moments as well as the coldness and detachment of the man who killed her. We must also respect their sharing the letter with the public as a conscious choice. How are we to read this letter? With both the horrific understatement of Kathy's pain and the suggestion that Kathy fought for her life, the document may best be viewed as a literary premonition of the "creepshot" photos taken by present-day campus predators after sexual assaults, "accidentally provid[ing] hard evidence in cases where 'she' was unconscious and cannot testify to what happened" (Oliver 9). In this case, however, the evidence was sent not to fellow conspirators, but to secondary victims, and Kathy was not unconscious, but dead.

A letter is not a photographic record, but this text exposes how perverse it is to perpetuate a self-serving myth of mercy for Whitman's violence. In the absence of an autopsy, it has been disturbingly easy to employ language aestheticizing Kathy's final moments. To acknowledge this epistolary artifact does not necessitate re-indulging the pornography of its author, but instead demands that we recognize intimate violence without airbrushed or "star crossed" verbiage that spares only the murderer—and us—rather than the victim or her family. After half a century, we should be shocked that a "creepshot" is necessary to disrupt how we elide or abject intimate murders through the gendered norms of true crime narratives. As authored for the intimate audience of grieving parents (and "with a love as thought [sic] you were my own […] please forgive me, if you can"), the letter is a summative exhibit of "courtliness and sadism" (Select Letters).

Conclusion

Narrative erasure of domestic injury or killing in American stories of public violence perpetuates a social injustice: repeated silencing of private victims who are usually women. We must reconsider how "softened" or selective depictions only make women's deaths more palatable, especially at the hands of men who claim to love them. Mid-century sexism may appear quaint when we compare it to the misogyny expressed so freely in contemporary social media forums, but we have inherited its violent legacy. Fifty years after Whitman murdered his wife and mother before ascending the UT tower to shoot at strangers, American voters elected to our highest public office a man caught on tape bragging about grabbing women "by the p*ssy" (Mathis-Lilley). Attitudes that degraded, ranked, and separated women more than a generation ago continue to impact daily lived experience in ordinary domestic spaces—in bedrooms, offices, and on college campuses—whether or not anyone points or shoots a gun. Importantly, gendered entitlement transcends political identification, as demonstrated by the "volatile" and abusive background of James T. Hodgkinson, who in June 2017 shot at Republican congressmen practicing on a baseball field (Turkewitz, Stolberg, Eligon, and Blinder).

Domestic terror is a matter of women's lives and public health, and it is past time to notice the connection between what happens, how we talk about it, and what we are able to remember. Writing of an estimated sixty-six thousand women killed by men every year, Rebecca Solnit refers to femicide as an ultimate erasure: "Such deaths often come after years or decades of being silenced or erased in the home, in daily life, by threat and violence. Some get erased a little at a time, some all at once. Some reappear" (71). Kathy has been able to "reappear" because her brother, Nelson, protected the primary documents that preserved his sister's voice and perspective. When we do not question how and why domestic violence is subordinated to public spectacle, we unintentionally perpetuate the abuser or killer's perspective about when and how women's lives and deaths matter. We must re-attune our awareness so that gendered and sexualized violence no longer seems, by distorted comparison, a minor detail or narrative footnote, despite the reality of its massive and continued collective impact.

17

Male Privilege and Societal Expectations Also Harm Men

Harris O'Malley

Harris O'Malley is a blogger and dating coach who runs the blog Dr. Nerdlove.

While women's bodies have long been scrutinized and held to impossible standards by men, Harris O'Malley argues that these unreachable standards of beauty and the harsh judgments they bring about are an issue for both men and women. But instead of these impossible standards for men being imposed by women, O'Malley asserts that men are subjected to the judgments of other men. Because of how male bodies appear in movies, TV shows, and on social media, men have unrealistic expectations about how they should appear, which leads to dysmorphia, low self esteem, and eating disorders. It also reinforces normative male gender roles and hypermasculinity.

Over the last couple of weeks, some news stories were brought to my attention that illustrate a problem I've been observing for a few years now.

The first was the latest in a long line of Photoshopping scandals. What made this interesting was that rather than some already-stick-thin female model being slimmed down even further or women of color having their skin lightened or their features made to look more caucasian, the subject in question was Justin Bieber.

"The New (and Impossible) Standards of Male Beauty," by Harris O'Malley, Dr. NerdLove, January 26, 2015. Reprinted by permission.

The website BreatheHeavy.com released what were supposedly unretouched photos of the Bieb—photos that suggested that Bieber's muscles and package got a Photoshop-based enlargement. Of course, Bieber's legal team went into overdrive, insisting that the "before" pictures were the altered ones and forced BreatheHeavy to retract them.

The other was an article in *Esquire UK*, where the author decided to spend three months in a quest to become—in his words—"totally ripped."

What strikes me about these stories is how they play into a new and pernicious narrative—the new standards for male beauty and how the quest to live up to them has been taking a deadly toll on men.

The Beauty Myth vs. the "Spornosexual"

In his article "The Rise and Rise of the Spornosexual," writer Max Olesker decided he wanted to explore what he saw as the new trend in young men—predominantly men in their early 20s, but many ranging up to their 50s—to sport bodies reminiscent of modern porn-stars, sports heroes and of course, movie stars. To many men, the lean-yet-jacked look has become de rigueur—the *ne plus ultra* of masculinity.

Of course, it's hard *not* to feel that way when it seems like every time you turn around, another shirtless man with 4% body fat and abs like *phwoar* is staring at you from television and movie screens, in every advertisement and video game that comes down the pike.

In what seems like a sick parody of gender equity, men hear more and more about fitness "success" stories from other men. Hugh Jackman tweets his workouts to get into superheroic shape with "fitspo" slogans like "if the bar ain't bending, you ain't lifting." Chris Pratt—having gone from chubby schlub to wash-board-ab-bedecked guardian of the galaxy—gets asked over and over about how he achieved his transformation. Zac Efron traded in an almost feminine beauty in his younger days to look like something that—quoting Seth Rogan's character in *Neighbors*—a gay man designed in a laboratory.

When you browse Tumblr or Pinterest, you can't help but see women drooling over Chris Evans as Captain America or Chris Hemsworth as Thor or the men of *Magic Mike* oiled up and strutting their stuff. In Hollywood, being built has become mandatory—even from people who aren't typically action stars. The everyman hero—think Bruce Willis in *Die Hard*, Will Smith, Keanu Reeves—the man who's athletic and in shape but still someone you might see at work, is dead. Now to be a movie star means having visible muscle striations in your pecs and a perfect runner's girdle pointing at the family jewels. If you're going to be a leading man in the hottest movies and TV shows—your Supermen, your Thors, your Arrows, even *romantic comedies*—you can't just look *good* with your shirt off, you have to look *perfect*.

The cruel irony, of course, is that men are now feeling the same pressures that *women* have been feeling for generations—to conform to an incredibly *specific* form of beauty. And of course, those who *don't* measure up are taught that they're failures—that they are inherently less desirable, even less *manly*, than the shiny-chested, leaned out Dolce and Gabana model. At a time when men *already* feel sexually invisible and desperate for validation (or even *acknowledgement*), being told that being sexy means being lean *and* jacked at all costs.

Welcome to the Beauty Myth boys. Hope you survive the experience.

The Hypermasculine Origins of the Beauty Standard

"Is that what a real man is supposed to look like?" Tyler Durden asks, pointing at an underwear ad—perfectly airbrushed abs hovering over tiny tighty-whities. In *Fight Club*, this is a moment of supreme irony; Tyler, of course, is played by Brad Pitt whose lean build is the Platonic ideal that Olesker and others strive for. He *already* looks like that model—better, some might say.

Of course, the other irony is that Tyler Durden is the manifestation of the nameless protagonist's id; he is *literally* the hypermasculine ideal that Ed Norton's character wishes he could be. Small wonder that he's also the representation of what men feel they're "supposed" to be.

The ideal man—the peak of male beauty we demand others conform to—falls in line with the tropes of hypermasculinity and traditional gender roles. You have to be tall—short men aren't "men" after all. You have to be lean, as lean as possible, because being fat means that you're lazy and pampered and a *man* is active. You have to be muscular because men are *strong*. Men are *fighters*. And of course, you have to be *virile*, because men who don't get b*tches just aren't *men*. Man as protector. Man as provider. Man as warrior.

We see these men lionized in television and film, on magazine covers and billboards—a look and lifestyle that is *literally* marketed to us. Gerard Butler's Leonidas in *300* is the cinematic ur-example— you don't get much more alpha than the totally jacked king of the Spartans—but the Internet provides its own real-life swole-models. Witness the so-called "King of Instagram" (there's that "alpha" leader title again), Dan Bilzerian. His Instagram account is photo after photo of Bilzerian shooting guns, partying with porn stars, lounging around his mansion and private jet.

Those pictures all carry the ironic echo of Tyler Durden: "All the ways you wish you could be, that's me. I look like you wanna look, I f**k like you wanna f**k, I am smart, capable, and most importantly, I am free in all the ways that you are not."

Yes, we're told. This *is* what a "real man" is supposed to look like. So start catching up, wuss.

See, despite what we tell ourselves, the male beauty standard isn't about what *women* think men should look like; it's brought onto us by *other men*.

Male Beauty and the Impossible Body

The problem is that this ideal body is almost impossible to achieve. Olesker inadvertently points out an unspoken truth: that gaining (and maintaining) the perfect masculine body has to be your *job*. In his quest for ultimate male beauty, Olesker has to eat and work out on a schedule so rigid that he's forcing himself to scarf down chicken breasts on the bus as he scrambles to make it to the next work out. It's one thing when you're a writer being paid to do a feature or a CEO who can dictate his own hours and schedule; it's another when you're working a standard 8-5 in a cubicle with only a 20 to 30 minute break for lunch and an hour's commute each way.

Those movie stars and models are literally being *paid* to work out and eat "clean"—usually at levels that the average joe can never meet. Neither are they paying for the meals or the nutritionists, or the trainers or the gym-time; the studios pay for it all, often delivering the food to their stars in order to maintain their workout schedules. Jason Momoa was eating 56 chicken breasts a *week* in order to play Khal Drogo. Chris Evans, Chris Pratt and Hugh Jackman all were putting in multiple 90+ minute work outs *each day* to get into shape for the movies. And this is *before* they set foot in front of the camera; getting ready for filming usually involves intense dehydration to make those muscles and veins pop, pushing diuretics and sweating out the last drops in order to get that perfect look. Even their *height* is frequently an illusion. Robert Downey Jr. is 5'8" and Tom Cruise is 5'7"—they just appear taller on camera by the magic of apple boxes and convenient ditches.

What also goes unmentioned is the secret weapon: testosterone and human-growth-hormone injections. What, you thought Hugh Jackman—*in his 40s*—got that vascular just by choking down chicken breasts?

Even then, those perfect muscles and ideal male beauty get an assist. Just as with women, those men are given a boost with some traditional Hollywood and Madison Avenue magic— carefully planned lighting, artfully applied make-up and, of course, Photoshop.

Moreover, even the celebrities—again, whose *job* it is to model the ideal—don't look like this year round. Stephen Amell looks like a Greek god (and, incidentally, sends me to the gym) every time he takes his shirt off to do the salmon ladder, but when he's *not* filming, he goes back to a more normal shape. Yes, he's still fit—again, his full-time job is to get camera-ready within eight weeks—but he doesn't look like Ollie Queen.

But the impossible male beauty doesn't look "fit," he looks "perfect" at all times … no matter the cost.

The High Price of Perfection

As I mentioned earlier, the pressure for men to measure up to this impossible ideal is a cruel parody of gender equality; we're rapidly approaching the point where men and women are *equally f**ked up* about our bodies. Just as women have for generations—since the invention of the daguerrotype, some say—men are starting to pay the price for male beauty.

Body dysmorphic disorder is on the rise in men. Studies have found that nearly half of *all* men are dissatisfied with their bodies and up to a quarter of people suffering from eating disorders are men.

What makes it even more patently absurd is the sheer damage that we do to ourselves trying to achieve and maintain that ideal look. 5% body fat *is not natural* in humans and comes with immense health risks. The stress on the body—from the unnatural level of body fat, the intensity of the workouts and the pressure on the psyche—can damage one's internal organs and weaken the immune system, leaving them vulnerable to disease. The cheats that many people use in order to maintain their bodies—taking ephedrine to counteract those beer-binges—can cause immeasurable damage as well.

And when I say "impossible" body, I mean it. Having the "perfect" body isn't just built in the gym or on the dinner plate, it's built in the womb. Genetics and bone structure dictate far more than can be achieved via workouts. The barrel-chested guy with the short waist (like, er, me) is never going to have the swimmer's build. The ectomorph isn't going to get the swole arms and chest of Brad Pitt. If you don't have the right combination of genes, you can work out as hard as you want, starve yourself as much as you can and *still* not get those picture perfect abs.

And this is without getting into the *other* issues such as food availability, hormonal balances and more that affect health and weight loss.

As a result, we end up with higher levels of depression and self-loathing. When we mock the "fat, cheeto-dust-covered nerd" we perpetuate this hate. We continue the idea that there's only *one* way to be attractive, that there's only *one* way to be a man. And when we feel that we can't measure up … there's a price to be paid.

But attractiveness isn't about *looks* or impossible standards of male beauty. It's a *matrix*—it's in how you act, in how you dress, in how you make others *feel*. It's in loving *yourself*, no matter whether you look like Zac Efron or Seth Rogen.

Yes, there are body types we all enjoy looking at. But appreciating them doesn't mean that this is the *only* type that we want. It's possible to enjoy staring at Chris Pratt in *Guardians of the Galaxy* and still prefer Chris Pratt in *Parks and Rec*. And yes, there will always be shallow people who insist that physical beauty is the only thing that matters. We call these people a**holes. And why would you want to date an a**hole in the first place?

Be fit, sure. Be healthy. But fit and healthy—just like beauty— comes in more than one shape.

18

Male Privilege Begins at Home

Usha Ram, Lisa Strohschein, and Kirti Gaur

Usha Ram is affiliated with the Centre for Global Health Research at St. Michael's Hospital in Toronto and the Department of Public Health and Mortality Studies at the International Institute for Population Sciences in Mumbai. Lisa Strohschein is associated with the University of Alberta in Edmonton, Canada. Kirti Gaur is also affiliated with the Department of Public Health and Mortality Studies.

According to the research presented in this viewpoint, male privilege is an entrenched aspect of society, and through looking at gender socialization in Indian households it becomes clear that these beliefs and behaviors often tend to begin at home. Furthermore, these childhood experiences can have long-term impacts on women's mental health, with significantly higher rates of mental health issues found among women who were subjected to violence or subjugation as children. Interestingly, higher rates of mental health issues were also found among men who were exposed to these stressors, suggesting that the ways families socialize children have wide-reaching impacts.

L isted as one of the eight Millennium Development Goals, the goal of ameliorating gender inequality and empowering women is well recognized as a critical tool for advancing population health, improving life chances, and bringing economic prosperity

"Gender Socialization: Differences between Male and Female Youth in India and Associations with Mental Health," by Usha Ram, Lisa Strohschein, and Kirti Gaur, Hindawi International Journal of Population Research, April 27, 2014, https://www.hindawi.com/journals/ijpr/2014/357145/. Licensed under CC BY 3.0.

to low- and middle-income countries. Nonetheless, the obstacles to achieving this goal are daunting, given that gender inequality is often entrenched at all levels of society and, thus, requires changing both institutional structures and individual behaviours. That is, gendered norms govern what is deemed to be acceptable behaviour for the sexes and become the basis upon which girls and women throughout the world are systematically given fewer resources and opportunities than boys and men. When these restrictions are condoned by political and legal systems, women and girls become powerless to protect themselves from harm and are made vulnerable to disease, mental disorder, and death.

Linking these broad structural forces to individual health outcomes, however, requires researchers to pay greater attention to the microlevel processes that reproduce gender inequality. Moss effectively bridged macro- and microlevel processes by identifying the household as an important site of gendered practices, whereby members favour male children but curb opportunities and resources for female children. Moreover, she suggested that researchers need to integrate these linkages in a way that acknowledges their geographic and historical specificity and accounts for different life stages. These ideas, combined with stress process theory, comprise the theoretical basis of the current study.

Theoretical Context

While gender norms are broadly reinforced culturally and institutionally, it is within the household that children first learn about gender roles, equating maleness with power and authority and femaleness with inferiority and subservience. Boys learn how to exercise their authority over girls, whereas girls learn to submit. Consequently, gender socialization entails learning how to perform the behaviours that are consistent with one's gender. Moreover, both males and females are held to account for that performance, such that social sanctions follow when one engages in behaviour that deviates from what is expected for one's gender.

In India, households are a primary site in which male privilege and control over women are expressed. Despite being banned since 1994, selective abortion of female foetuses has become increasingly common and excess female mortality among children under age 5 years is seen in all parts of the country. With few lifestyle options outside of marriage, girls are expected to marry. Yet daughters often prove to be financially burdensome for families as they must produce a sizeable dowry to the husband's family (the practice of dowry also remains widespread despite antidowry laws since the 1960s). Because verifying her chastity is a critical step in the marriage process, families are careful to regulate all aspects of their daughters' lives, controlling where they go and what they may do. From an early age, Indian girls are told that their proper place is in the home, fulfilling domestic duties and attending to the needs of men, whereas males learn that they are superior to women and must exercise authority over them.

Gender socialization occurs not only through the acquisition of gender-appropriate behaviours, but also through observing adults in the household, who are role models to children. When the household is characterized by family violence, children encounter another form of gender socialization. That is, children who witness fathers beating their mothers may become conditioned to accept violence in their relationships. Research in India has already established that violence is transmitted across generations, showing that married men who, as children, witnessed their father beating their mother were significantly more likely to condone and commit acts of violence against their own wives.

By positing that chronic strains and stressful life events threaten an individual's adaptive capacity, stress process theory provides a useful conceptual framework for linking patterns of gender socialization to the mental health of male and female youth in India. First, stress process recognizes that stressors are generally harmful for the mental health of male and female youth. Thus, witnessing violence between parents and experiencing parental beatings are well-established predictors of mental health problems for both male and female youth. Similarly, barriers that inhibit efforts to become more independent may create frustration and despair for youth, generating mental health problems regardless of gender. At the same time, however, it must be recognized that exposure to these stressors is not random, with females more likely to encounter barriers to independence because of their sex.

Second, it is likely that gender unequal practices within households produce their intended effect. When obstacles on the path to success are removed for males without regard to the cost for female children, male children should benefit while female children must work harder to keep up. Thus, in households where there is greater gender inequality, male youth should be expected to report fewer mental health problems. For female youth, living in a household with higher levels of gender inequality should be associated with greater mental health problems.

Finally, stress process recognizes that stressors arise when male and female youth engage in behaviour that is inconsistent with the expectations for their gender. For example, when male youth engage in domestic chores within the home, they are performing activities that are coded as feminine. In a society that clearly demarcates differences between the sexes, youth whose conduct is inconsistent with one's gender are at risk for social sanctions. Thus, it is likely that performing sex-atypical tasks will be associated with greater mental health problems.

Although Indian society is marked by deep gender inequality, evidence linking gender socialization to mental health problems among youth is sorely lacking. Indeed, there are only a few studies that evaluate the links between gender socialization and youth mental health. In their analysis of predictors of common mental disorders in Indian youth aged 15–24 from state of Goa, Fernandes et al. found that older youth who had reported being beaten by a teacher or family member in the past three months were at greater risk for common mental disorder. Pillai and colleagues found that youth living in Goa who engaged in independent decision-making were less likely to be suicidal than youth who were unable to make independent decisions. The study further noted frequent verbal or physical abuse by parents, low parental support, and gender-based discrimination as significant predictors of mental health problems among Goan youth. This study, however, narrowly evaluated gender-discriminatory practices with two questions asking whether the youth were treated differently or restrained from certain activities because of their gender.

This small amount of evidence on the Indian context lends support to the idea that gender socialization is linked to mental health problems in male and female youth. As such, the current study had two aims. The first goal was to describe differences in gender socialization by comparing youth-reported family experiences, independence, and gender role attitudes. It is hypothesized that male youth will experience more freedom and privileges than female youth in their households. Differences in recognizing gender-discriminatory practices within households and gender egalitarian attitudes between male and female youth were also examined.

The second goal was to apply insights from stress process to test whether gender socialization was associated with mental health problems among male and female youth. Experiences that are stressful (exposure to family violence and restrictions to independence) are hypothesized to be equally detrimental to the mental health of male and female youth. Because gender-discriminatory practices afford advantages to males while simultaneously blocking opportunities for females, it was hypothesized that higher levels of gender-discriminatory practices within household will be associated with fewer mental health problems among male youth. Conversely, higher levels of gender-discriminatory practices should be associated with greater mental health problems among female youth. Finally, it was hypothesized that behaviours that contravene gender-specific norms, such as when females engage in male-typed chores and males perform tasks that are coded feminine, will be associated with worse mental health.

[...]

Results

[...]

Family life experiences were significant predictors of mental health problems among females; females whose families engaged in gender-discriminatory practices reported significantly more mental health problems than those whose families did not engage in such practices. Females who performed household tasks outside the home reported significantly more mental health problems than those who did not. Females who witnessed parental violence reported significantly more mental health problems than those who did not. Females who had been beaten by a parent after the age of 12 as well as those who could not remember being beaten reported significantly more mental health than those who had not been beaten.

Females who had independent decision-making in none or in only one of the three areas reported significantly more mental health problems than females who exercised independent decision-making in all three areas. Females who could neither confront nor express their opinion reported mental health problems that were, on average, 15% higher than those who could do both. Mental health problems were significantly higher for females who could go unescorted to one of three places inside their village/ neighbourhood and for females who could not go to any place inside their village/neighbourhood unescorted relative to females with no restrictions. Compared with females who subscribed to egalitarian gender role attitudes on six or more items, females who subscribed to egalitarian attitudes on four or fewer items reported significantly more mental health problems.

As was the case with models for female youth, many control variables were significant in bivariate models; however, in multivariable analyses, not all remained significant. Each additional year of age was associated with a 3% increase in mental health problems for male youth. Urban males reported 18% fewer mental health problems than rural males, whereas males in western and northern regions reported 30–45% more mental health problems than those in southern regions. Males from a scheduled tribe reported significantly more mental health problems than general castes males. Compared to single/never married males, married males currently living with their spouse and those married but no gauna reported significantly fewer mental health problems. Relative to males from the wealthiest households, males from the lowest three household wealth quintiles reported significantly more mental health problems.

Males who grew up in families engaging in gender-discriminatory practices that favoured sons reported significantly fewer mental health problems than those who grew up in families that did not engage in gender-discriminatory practices. Males who engaged in domestic tasks inside the home had on average 16% more mental health problems than those who did not. Males who did domestic tasks outside [the] home reported 27% fewer mental health problems than those who did not. Males who witnessed parental violence reported on average 28% more mental health problems than those who never witnessed parental violence. Male youth who had ever been beaten by parent(s) after the age of 12 reported on average 12% more mental health problems than those who had not been beaten.

Males who could either express their opinions or confront others and males who could neither express nor confront reported significantly more mental health problems than those who could do both. Compared to males with no restrictions on their mobility inside their village/neighbourhood, mental health problems were 25% higher for males who could go unescorted to one of the three places and 73% higher for males who could not go unescorted to any place. Males who were able to go to two of the three places outside their village/neighbourhood reported significantly more mental health problems than males with unlimited mobility. Males with no access to money reported significantly more mental health problems than those who had both access and control. Males who subscribed to four or fewer egalitarian gender role attitudes reported significantly more mental health problems than those who subscribed to six or more.

Discussion

Poised to have one of the largest pools of young people in the world, youth will play a pivotal role in building the future of the Indian society. As youth enter adult roles and prepare to parent the next generation, there is a pressing need to understand how gender socialization has shaped their experiences and how these experiences are connected to their mental well-being. As the first to address these issues in the Indian context, the current study makes the following contributions.

First, findings confirm that fewer female youth in India enjoy the same privileges afforded male youth, providing a comprehensive portrait of their family lives. Both male and female youth indicated that gender-discriminatory practices within their households were common, with sons given preference in education, freedom to roam, and household tasks. In all instances, male youth were more likely to identify gender-discriminatory practices within households than female youth. This is a troubling finding as it suggests that female youth lack awareness that they are disadvantaged by their gender.

Female youth also faced greater barriers to independence than male youth as they were less likely to engage in independent decision-making in their day-to-day lives, faced greater restrictions on their mobility, and lacked access to money. To the extent that these are key stepping stones for success in adulthood, observed deficits among female youth are likely to limit upward mobility and contribute to persisting gender inequalities throughout adulthood.

Despite household practices that favoured male youth over female youth, mobility, independent decision-making, and access to money were not universal among male youth. Fewer than half of male youth could express their opinion to elders (aside from parents) or confront others who had wronged them. Most male youth did not have access to money. Thus, there is considerable room for improving independent behaviour among male youth as well.

Finally, a greater proportion of females than males subscribed to gender-egalitarian attitudes. This finding is interesting when contrasted with the finding that a greater proportion of males than females identified gender-discriminatory practices within households. What this suggests is that while males generally recognize that females are not afforded the same privileges as males, they do not see these arrangements as problematic.

A second contribution of this study is that it confirms links between gender socialization and youth mental health. Indeed, drawing on stress process, support was found for all three hypotheses linking gender socialization to the mental health of male and female youth. First, the results of this study show that stressful experiences are harmful to the mental health of both male and female youth. Consistent with prior research youth experiencing a parental beating reported more mental health problems than those who did not experience violence at the hands of their parents. Similarly, restrictions to youth mobility and expressing themselves to others were associated with mental health problems for both male and female youth. Although females face more barriers to independence than males, greater independence is linked to better mental health for both sexes.

Importantly, this study shows the association between gender-discriminatory practices and mental health operates in different directions for male and female youth. For male youth, the higher the level of household gender-discriminatory practices, the lower the amount of mental health problems. In contrast, females reported higher mental health problems as the number of gender-discriminatory practices in their households increased. The household environment emerges as a key setting in which gender inequality becomes insinuated in the fabric of social life, with corresponding influences on mental health and well-being. As such, this study is able to connect the microlevel practices of the household to the diverging destinies of male and female youth and their mental well-being.

Finally, consistent with the hypothesis that violating gender norms would be associated with worse mental health, performing household tasks inside the home was associated with more mental health problems for male youth, whereas female youth who performed chores outside the home reported more mental health problems (gender consistent behaviour in these areas was unrelated or associated with better mental health). To the extent that gender boundaries are rigorously policed in Indian society, it is clear that engaging in gender-inconsistent behaviour was associated with mental health problems for both male and female youth.

Although not the focus of this study, results also affirm sociodemographic characteristics including caste and wealth quintiles as predictors of mental health. Given that most demographic variables were associated with mental health problems in bivariate analyses, the social patterning of mental health problems remains an important upstream factor that requires further investigation in the Indian context.

Organizations to Contact

The editors have compiled the following list of organizations concerned with the issues debated in this book. The descriptions are derived from materials provided by the organizations. All have publications or information available for interested readers. The list was compiled on the date of publication of the present volume; the information provided here may change. Be aware that many organizations take several weeks or longer to respond to inquiries, so allow as much time as possible.

American Association of University Women (AAUW)
1310 L Street NW, Suite 1000
Washington, DC 20005
phone: (202) 785–7700
email: connect@aauw.org
website: www.aauw.org

The American Association of University Women, founded in 1881, is concerned with closing the pay gap for women across the United States through research, education, and advocacy. They lobby for public policy measures that ensure equality in the workplace, conduct research that analyzes gender equity issues in education and the workplace, and lead educational programs and workshops.

Gay and Lesbian Alliance Against Defamation (GLAAD)
104 W. 29th Street, #4
New York, NY 10001
phone: (212) 629–3322
website: www.glaad.org

The Gay and Lesbian Alliance Against Defamation was founded in 1985 in response to the vilification of LGBTQ+ individuals in the media during the AIDS crisis. Today, the organization works with entertainment and news media to promote the positive portrayal of all LGBTQ+ people and to share their stories.

The National Center for Men
117 Pauls Path #531
Coram, NY 11727
phone: (631) 476–2115
email: info@nationalcenterformen.org
website: www.nationalcenterformen.org

The National Center for Men promotes men's equal rights and advocates for men who have been hurt by sex discrimination. They focus on father's rights, male victims of domestic violence, and male divorcees. The organization also provides counseling and educational programs for men struggling with any of these issues. They believe that men should be afforded the same rights and freedoms that feminism has given women.

National Coalition for Men
932 C Street, Suite B
San Diego, CA 92101
phone: (619) 231–1909
email: ncfm@ncfm.org
website: www.ncfm.org

The National Coalition for Men was founded in 1977 and advocates for men's rights and combats anti-male stereotypes. They believe that men do not have all of the privileges the media and scholarship claim they do, and that men suffer as victims of paternity cases, false rape accusations, and sexual assault. They focus on activism through educational services, outreach, and litigation.

National Organization for Men Against Sexism (NOMAS)

3700 E. 17th Avenue
Denver, CO 80206
phone: (720) 466–3882
email: info@nomas.org
website: www.nomas.org/

The National Organization for Men Against Sexism is a pro-feminist, pro-LGBTQ+, anti-racist organization that aims to challenge toxic masculinity and male privilege. The organization compiles research and resources related to domestic violence, men's mental health, homophobia, and more. NOMAS also provides leadership for an anti-sexist men's movement.

National Organization for Women (NOW)

1100 H Street NE #300
Washington, DC 20002
phone: (202) 628–8669
website: www.now.org/

The National Organization for Women is a grassroots activism campaign founded in 1966 during the second wave of feminism. It has hundreds of chapters across the United States and is committed to intersectional activism, including women's reproductive rights; political, social, and economic equality; racial equality; and LGBTQ+ rights.

National Women's History Museum

205 S. Whiting Street, Suite 254
Alexandria, VA 22304
phone: (703) 461–1920
email: info@womenshistory.org
website: www.womenshistory.org

The National Women's History Museum is an online educational institution devoted to promoting balanced historical scholarship and preserving women's vital and diverse contributions to history.

They do this through digital exhibitions, educational resources, and occasional events. They also offer speakers by request.

National Women's Law Center
11 Dupont Circle, NW, #800
Washington, DC 20036
phone: (202) 588–5180
website: www.nwlc.org

The National Women's Law Center strives to promote laws and policies that ensure equality for women and families. They conduct research, analysis, advocacy, and public education programs. In the past 40 years, they have helped secure laws that protect the jobs of pregnant women, raised minimum wages, and enforced Title IX.

Organization for Black Struggle
1401 Rowan Avenue
St. Louis, MO 63112
phone: (314) 367–5959
email: contactus@obs-stl.org
website: www.obs-stl.org/

The Organization for Black Struggle aims to eliminate all forms of oppression and exploitation from society, and it considers sexism and male privilege a part of that. Although the organization is focused on bringing social, cultural, economic, and political justice to the black community, they also identify LGBTQ+ rights and gender equality as central to the struggle to end oppression. They offer opportunities for political activism through canvassing and provide educational resources for victims of police brutality.

Women's Global Empowerment Fund
PO Box 6283
Denver, CO 80206
phone: (303) 520–7656
email: microfund@gmail.com
website: www.wgefund.org

The Women's Global Empowerment Fund aims to provide women around the world with the educational and practical resources to support themselves. They offer programs that teach finance, literacy, and political leadership. They believe the best way to curb sexism, poverty, and male domination is to empower women to take charge in their own homes and communities.

Bibliography

Books

Margaret L. Andersen and Patricia Hill Collins, eds., *Race, Class, and Gender: An Anthology*. Belmont, CA: Wadsworth Publishing Inc., 2004.

Francine D. Blau, Marianna A. Ferber, and Anne E. Winkler, *The Economics of Women, Men, and Work*. London, UK: Pearson Series in Economics, 2013.

Ta-Nehisi Coates, *Between the World and Me*. New York, NY: Spiegel & Grau, 2015.

Ellis Cose, *A Man's World: How Real Is Male Privilege—and How High Is Its Price?* New York, NY: HarperCollins, 1995.

Nancy E. Dowd, *The Man Question: Male Subordination and Privilege*. New York, NY: New York University Press, 2010.

Warren Farrell, *Why Men Earn More*. New York, NY: American Management Association, 2005.

Joe R. Feagin and Eileen O'Brien, *White Men on Race: Power, Privilege, and the Shaping of Cultural Consciousness*. Boston, MA: Beacon Press, 2003.

Michael Flood and Judith Kegan Gardiner, *International Encyclopedia of Men and Masculinity*. New York, NY: Routledge, 2007.

Allan G. Johnson, *The Gender Knot: Unraveling Our Patriarchal Legacy*. Philadelphia, PA: Temple University Press, 2014.

Jackson Katz, *The Macho Paradox: Why Some Men Hurt Women and How All Men Can Help*. Naperville, IL: Sourcebooks, Inc., 2006.

Michael S. Kimmel, *Angry White Men: American Masculinity at the End of an Era*. New York, NY: Bold Type Books, 2017.

Michael S. Kimmel and Abby L. Ferber, eds., *Privilege: A Reader.* Boulder, CO: Westview Press, 2014.

Audre Lorde, *Sister Outsider: Essays and Speeches.* New York, NY: Crossing Press, 2007.

Cherríe Moraga and Gloria Anzaldúa, eds., *This Bridge Called My Back: Writings by Radical Women of Color.* Albany, NY: State University of New York Press, 2015.

C. J. Pascoe, *Dude, You're a Fag: Masculinity and Sexuality in High School.* Berkeley, CA: University of California Press, 2011.

Grayson Perry, *The Descent of Man.* New York, NY: Penguin Books, 2017.

Periodicals and Internet Sources

Charles M. Blow, "Checking My Male Privilege," *New York Times,* October 29, 2017. https://www.nytimes.com/2017/10/29/opinion/checking-my-male-privilege.html.

Tori DeAngelis, "Unmasking 'Racial Micro Aggressions,'" *American Psychological Association,* 2009. https://www.apa.org/monitor/2009/02/microaggression.aspx.

Stefani Dexaeris, "Are Women Innocent?" *Huffington Post,* February 29, 2016. https://www.huffingtonpost.com/entry/are-women-innocent_b_9331770?ec_carp=3208396805674560861.

Larry Elder, "'White Male Privilege,' RIP," *RealClearPolitics,* 2018. https://www.realclearpolitics.com/articles/2018/10/04/white_male_privilege_rip_138248.html.

Hannah Ellis-Petersen and Mark Sweney, "BBC Women 'Furious but Not Surprised' by Gender Pay Gap," *Guardian,* July 21, 2017. https://www.theguardian.com/media/2017/

jul/21/bbc-women-furious-and-not-surprised-by-gender-pay-gap.

Tal Fortgang, "Why I'll Never Apologize for My White Male Privilege," *Time,* May 2, 2014. http://time.com/85933/why-ill-never-apologize-for-my-white-male-privilege/.

Rose Hackman, "'I Didn't Choose to Be Straight, White, and Male': Are Modern Men the Suffering Sex?" *Guardian,* September 5, 2016. https://www.theguardian.com/world/2016/sep/05/straight-while-men-suffering-sex-feminism?CMP=twt_gu&CMP=aff_1432&awc=5795_1546508030_6d5fd259c14cbe75f296c9cc38ca4c7f.

Billy Doidge Kilgore, "I Didn't Understand Male Privilege Until I Became a Stay-at-Home Dad," *Washington Post,* March, 26, 2018. https://www.washingtonpost.com/news/parenting/wp/2018/03/26/being-a-stay-at-home-dad-raised-my-awareness-of-male-privilege-and-i-cant-ignore-it/?utm_term=.d46b216a111e.

Thomas Page McBee, "My Voice Got Deeper. Suddenly, People Listened," August 9, 2018, *New York Times.* https://www.nytimes.com/2018/08/09/style/transgender-men-voice-change.html.

Peggy McIntosh, "White Privilege and Male Privilege: A Personal Account of Coming to See Correspondences Through Work in Women's Studies," the National SEED Project. https://nationalseedproject.org/Key-SEED-Texts/white-privilege-and-male-privilege

Frank Newport, "Slight Preference for Having Boy Children Persists in US," *Gallup,* July 5, 2018. https://news.gallup.com/poll/236513/slight-preference-having-boy-children-persists.aspx.

Brendan O'Neill, "I Hate to Break It to Feminists, but 'White Male Privilege' Is a Myth," *Spectator,* January 5, 2016, https://blogs.spectator.co.uk/2016/01/i-hate-to-break-it-to-feminists-but-white-male-privilege-is-a-myth/.

Bedford Palmer, "Men's Intersectional Relationship to Male Privilege: Ending #MeToo Experiences Starts with Men Being More Aware of Their Privilege," *Psychology Today,* January 1, 2018. https://www.psychologytoday.com/us/blog/who-we-ought-be/201801/men-s-intersectional-relationship-male-privilege.

James St. James, "These 25 Examples of Male Privilege from a Trans Guy's Perspective Really Prove the Point," *Everyday Feminism Magazine,* May 30, 2015. https://everydayfeminism.com/2015/05/male-privilege-trans-men/.

Kim Susser, "Gender-Based Violence and Male Privilege," *Huffington Post,* October 15, 2015. https://www.huffingtonpost.com/entry/gender-based-violence-and_b_8305760?ec_carp=5727023717460157834.

Index